T0196939

This is It

This is It

THE REAL THING

Ward D. McGill

THIS IS IT
THE REAL THING

iUniverse books may be ordered through booksellers or by contacting:

iUniverse
1663 Liberty Drive
Bloomington, IN 47403
www.iuniverse.com
1-800-Authors (1-800-288-4677)

ISBN: 978-1-5320-5467-9 (sc)
ISBN: 978-1-5320-5470-9 (e)

Library of Congress Control Number: 2018912377

Print information available on the last page.

iUniverse rev. date: 01/21/2019

Contents

Foreword.. ix

Acknowledgments xi

My Flag.. xiii

Chapter 1   Introduction To Combat 1

Chapter 2   The Attack 21

Chapter 3   Debacle At Herrlisheim 47

Chapter 4   Colmar Pocket...90

Chapter 5   Sterling-Wendel...107

Chapter 6   Drive To The Rhine & Beyond 122

Chapter 7   Attack On Nassig 151

Chapter 8   Hettstadt-Finis La Guerre 159

This Is "It", The Real Thing

Chronicling the activities of B Co., 66th Armored Infantry Battalion,

Ward D. McGill
B/66, 12th Armored Div.

Foreword

T his is to be a story about the war. "What war?" you may ask? "Any war." I might reply. The human emotions, pain and suffering of combatants have been universal since the first man took up a stone and threw it at his adversary to commit premeditated homicide.

Actually, this is a story about WWII. War as I knew it. Not the war as a whole, but the small part in which I participated.

The part that a single soldier plays in the big picture is, of course, insignificant. Each day, for every one of those hundreds of combat men is filled with many and varied emotions. These emotions affect some more than others. It is my object in writing this, to try to convey some of the feelings, pleasures, fears and dislikes of the front line soldier.

It is impossible to describe a war. You can relate all the details, but until you have heard, seen, felt and smelled its loathsomeness, it is remote and unreal.

This book may not be the most historically correct account of WWII, but it is the way that I remember it.

Acknowledgments

When my enemies are turned back, they shall fall and perish at thy presence. For thou hast maintained my right and my cause; thou satest in thy throne judging right.

Ps. 9:3&4 (KJV)

Thank you, mother, for your prayers!!

My Flag

Today I burned my flag.

Not before a jeering hissing crowd of unruly protesters, but in the quietness of my home.

It was an old and tattered emblem. A flag which had flown for many years in front of our home. It was torn and had evidence of loving stitches which my wife had applied in an effort to prolong its life. Earlier in the day, I had replaced the old flag on its staff with a new one. Bright and crisp it was. Beautiful in its own right. The old flag fell to the floor in a pitiful heap. It bore no semblance to the great nation and the freedom of its people which it had so nobly represented.

I placed the old flag in the family dumpster and turned to walk away. "Is this the way to dispose of the symbol of my country?" I asked myself. I was not sure. Tears came to my eyes as I reflected on what that old piece of cloth represented in my life. Years ago I had offered my life on behalf of that flag and the country that it represents. I was wounded, not killed, and my grateful nation has done everything in its power to let me know that my sacrifice is deeply appreciated.

I called my local Disabled American Veterans club to determine the proper way of disposing of a retired flag. "Burn it," I was told. Down to the garage I went and retrieved my flag from the dumpster. All this time I was musing, "I didn't know a flag meant so much to me." Perhaps this is the reason that I cannot recite the Pledge of Allegiance or sing the National Anthem through without choking up.

As I lit the fireplace and placed the flag gently on the flame, I became tearful once more. I was alone with my flag. No one else was there to see the old veteran in the process of destroying the emblem of the country that he loves. Kneeling on one knee in front of the fireplace, I watched as the red, white and blue colors slowly disappeared and turned to ash. I remained there until the last bit of flame flickered and died.

The new flag is beautiful. It represents everything for which we fought. When we were 20, we didn't know what the word "freedom" meant. Now that we are older and have seen enough of the world to know what other countries are like compared to ours, we realize that what we fought for may then have been a dream but today is a reality.

I love my God, my family and my country. Without the latter, the freedom to worship as I please and to raise my family according to my convictions would be meaningless.

Let us never take our flag for granted or cease to cherish and protect the freedoms that it represents.

Ward McGill, January 22, 2002

My Flag

Major Battles Of Company B, 66th Armored Infantry Bn.

1. Maginot Line.
2. Herrlisheim
3. Colmar Pocket
4. Sterling-Wendel
5. Drive to the Rhine / Ludwigshaven
6. Nassig
7. Hettstedt

Chapter I

INTRODUCTION TO COMBAT

The war—that is the shooting war, started for me on the 5th day of December 1944. We were headed for the front, after spending about a week in our assembly area in Lunneville, France. The company was in convoy, moving steadily along the road when the sound of machine gun fire rose above the roar of tanks and half-tracks. I was acting as vehicle commander on our track, at the time. This particular vehicle mounted a fifty caliber machine gun, and it was my job to use it, should the need arise. When the sound of firing reached my ears, my first thoughts were that we had been ambushed. My reflexes? Well, to my shame, I hated to admit to the squad which had been entrusted to my care, was to duck, and duck I did. I finally steeled my nerves enough to raise my head above the turret. (I had decided to do or die, rather than risk the scorn of my buddies.) When my eyes did come above the edge of the turret, it was just in time to see a Jerry plane scurrying away down the valley, at tree top level. Tracer bullets from every direction were streaking after it. The plane looked just like the pictures we had been shown back in training. Apparently the fighter had strafed the rear elements of our convoy. No doubt the pilot realized that the flak wagons, with their heavy anti-aircraft guns would be up front with the tanks and half-tracks.

I also was aware that T/Sgt. Huff, our platoon Sgt. had reacted just as I did. He came up out of the gun turret of the half-track ahead of me at the same time I did.

A warm sense of relief was felt by all. Happy that helmeted and armed German soldiers were not swarming out of the woods beside our road.

This was the first time the enemy had shown himself. It was my first time under fire, and I had had a chance to study my reaction. Frankly, I was disappointed. Was this the way I was going to react whenever trouble broke?

The convoy continued on it's way for several hours, passing through towns that were in shambles. Hardly a building remained that did not have a shell hole in the roof, or wall. Most of the houses were roofless. The tile shingles of Alsace are not fastened by nails as are the shingled roofs with which we are familiar. Whenever a shell or bomb would land nearby, the whole roof would often raise up in one solid sheet, and them come crumbling and crashing to the ground in a pile of rubble.

About four o'clock that afternoon, the word got around that we were to relieve the Fourth Armored Division. This brought our morale up considerably. Any outfit which was considered good enough to replace the famous Fourth Armored, must be very good. It also left a feeling of apprehension. If the sector had been occupied by one of our crack armored outfits, we must be prepared to meet plenty of opposition. The enemy was not very apt to leave an outfit with the reputation of the Fourth sitting around with nothing to do. About three weeks later when the Belgium Bulge started, and the Fourth was swung into action to rescue the 101st Airborne Division, and punch the sagging battle line back into some semblance of a line, we realized why they had been moved.

It was this afternoon that I saw my first honest to goodness combat soldier. He was a boy of about twenty. I remember wondering how anyone could get so dirty and still claim to be in the United States Army. He grinned from ear to ear when he spotted our immaculate vehicles, our clean field jackets, and unsoiled helmets. "What outfit is this?", he grinned. "We're the Twelfth Armored, come up to relieve you guys", we answered, surveying wide-eyed his battle gear, which included grenades and rifle clips hanging from every portion of his apparel. "Where's the Krauts?" "I don't know" he answered, "but our tanks took off over that hill this morning like they were going someplace". Of course we plied him with many and varied questions, some of them no doubt, not too intelligent. Our conversation was interrupted by the signal to move on. Once more we were on our way up.

As we rolled along the muddy road, we passed half-tracks loaded with dirty, muddy, unshaven men. Some of the tracks were not very full; in fact some only held two or three men but every vehicle was mud spattered. Some bore the souvenirs of battle, German helmets and other equipment glorified the bumpers & grilles. These were men and machines which had grappled with the enemy and found that he was not invincible but that war was no child's game. We wondered what it took to give men that tired, haggard look that they all seemed to wear. Despite their grime and dirt, however, most of them could still smile, and many words of encouragement were spoken to us, such as "if you live through your first battle, you're sure to make it through the rest of the war", or "those Jerries aren't so tough boys, just keep your fannies down".

Several men from my squad, three to be exact, had been in the Fourth Armored back in Pine Camp, New York. You can imagine their pleasure in seeing men they had known back in the States. Many cheery greetings passed, as our train of vehicles rolled past small groups of engineers and doughboys along the road. Finally we came to a small

Luniville was our final staging area, before combat. Here we gave up our duffle bags with a lot of personal stuff. Cameras, civilian glasses and excess clothing. We were here around the first of December, 1944. Stayed 3 or 4 days in the gymnasium of a school. Possibly a college.

The town of Saar Union, is where Division Headquarters was located while we were committed to combat in the Maginot Line on December 7th. In contact with the enemy for about a week

We were assigned to Seventh Army reserve in this area until mid January, 1945

TABLE OF ORGANIZATION
1st RIFLE SQAD, 3rd RIFLE PLATOON B/66
December 7, 1944

SQUAD LEADER: Staff Sgt. George Dow
>   Evacuated with self inflicted wound
ASSISTANT SQUAD LEADER: Pfc. Ward McGill
>   Promoted to Sgt. and wounded in action

HALF-TRACK DRIVER: Tech. five, Sigismond Ryfinski
>   ASSISTANT   DRIVER/RIFLEMAN:
>   Pfc. Virl Birtch. Wounded in action.

RIFLEMAN: Pfc. Frank Chandler
RIFLEMAN: Pfc. John Kitchen
RIFLEMAN: Pfc. Dale Ell
>   Wounded in action & returned to duty.
RIFLEMAN: Pfc. Calvin Kuter
>   Evacuated with Traumatic Stress Disorder
RIFLEMAN: Pfc. Calvin Ganyard
RIFLEMAN: Pfc. Michael Drozd
>   Wounded in action, not evacuated.
RIFLEMAN: Pfc. Ralph Bratcher
RIFLEMAN: Allen Bark
>   Killed in action

Ward D. McGill

TABLE OF ORGANIZATION
THIRD RIFLE PLATOON, B COMPANY, 66th ARMORED
INFANTRY BATTALION
December 7, 1944

PLATOON COMMANDER: 2nd Lt. William H. Horrell
Promoted to Company Executive Officer

PLATOON LEADER: Tech Sgt. Glenn Huff
Promoted to 2nd Lt. & killed in action

1st RIFLE SQUAD LEADER: Staff Sgt. George Dow
Evacuated with a self-inflicted wound
ASSISTANT SQUAD LEADER: Pfc. Ward McGill
Promoted to Sgt. & wounded in action
2nd RIFLE SQUAD LEADER: Staff Sgt. Fischer
Evacuated with Traumatic Stress Disorder
ASSISTANT SQUAD LEADER: Sgt. Scott
Evacuated with apendicitis
3rd RIFLE SQUAD LEADER: Staff Sgt. Bernard Manion
Promoted to Tech. Sgt.
ASSISTANT SQUAD LEADER: Sgt. Robert Edwards
Promoted to Staff Sgt. & wounded in action
MACHINE GUN SQUAD LEADER: Staff Sgt. William McBride
ASSISTANT SQUAD LEADER: Sgt. Frank Szmoniac
Promoted to Staff Sgt. & killed in action
MORTAR SQUAD LEADER: Staff Sgt. Gene Sabin

muddy, badly battered village where our convoy was held up by a group of heavily loaded ambulances heading for the rear. They were crossing a narrow wooden bridge which had just been replaced by an engineer unit. Evidently there was a war on up ahead, these men didn't get hurt opening "C" rations.

Right here I'd like to introduce my squad to whomever it may concern. I am doing this for my own benefit as well as anyone who might read this. Time dulls one's memory and I'd like to remember these men. First, there was our squad leader, S/Sgt. George Dow, a soft spoken executive type of fellow who sported a pair of thick lens G.I. glasses. Next, in grade that is, was our driver T/5 Sigmund Ryfinski, a wild Polack or rather, Lithuanian from Syracuse, New York. If a strong wind was ever felt around our quarters or in our half track, you could usually be sure that "Rye" was talking. The rest of the squad, consisting of Pfc's and Pvt's were my very close buddy, Frank Chandler of Louisville, Kentucky; Calvin Ganyard of Medina, Ohio; John Kitchen of Dover Foxcroft, Maine; Dale Ell of Ohio; Michael Drodz of Pennsylvania; Allen Bark, the Division's "bad boy"; Ralph "Kid" Bratcher of Memphis, Tennessee; and Calvin Kuter of Wisconsin. Also included was our assistant driver, Virl Birtch of Idaho.

By the time dusk came upon us, our convoy was halted on what seemed to be an open road, although the terrain was hilly. As the darkness fell, we could see the flashes of shell bursts on the horizon and hear the roll of the big guns, like thunder during an electric storm. We were informed that we were to stay here all night, but that we should be ready to move at a minute's notice. The ground was too wet to lay our sleeping bags on, so most of the men tried to sleep sitting up in the vehicle, while the driver rolled his bag on the warm hood of the track. As for myself, I was determined to sleep, war or no war, so I made my bed on top of the other bed rolls in the rack on the back of the vehicle. I had no more than become settled and warm, than I heard the drone of an approaching plane. I knew it wasn't ours as the anti-aircraft guns all along our convoy were barking angrily and the shells were bursting directly over my bed, at least it seemed so to me. I was almost too tired to care if they came right into my sack. At any rate, the disturber was driven off, and when my shaking had subsided I finally slipped off into a blissful slumber.

The next morning I awakened to find a fine mist of rain falling. Rain always occurs where a war is being fought. Mud is mud, wherever it is found, but Alsatian mud seemed to be of its own special consistency. In the first place, instead of being ankle deep, it was knee deep, and whenever a piece of clothing touched it, that piece of cloth was immediately saturated and plastered with the stuff.

It was very gratifying to find that our kitchen crew was serving hot breakfast for us. This was a welcome change after the "K" rations which we had consumed the day before. As our company vehicles were still tactically dispersed, it was about a half mile to the chow truck. Of course we felt it was worth it. After spreading our vehicular camouflage net over our track, and posting a one man guard, the rest went happily down the road in a column, with rifles slung on shoulders and mess kits jingling. The meal was served in typical army style, with bread and butter on the bottom of the mess kit – on top of that came those luscious (hiss) dehydrated potatoes then fresh canned peas, with gravy on top. All of this was topped off with canned pears. This conglomeration mixed with ample amounts of fresh rain water, which was constantly falling, made the soldier who was eating it wish that he had a nice box of "K" rations.

When the meal, if it could be called that, was finished we straggled back to our vehicles through the mud and slush. The squad had no sooner put its mess gear away than a runner came down the road with orders for us to "stow all camouflage nets and all squad leaders report to the C.P. (Command Post, or Company Commander).

If the reader has ever tried rolling a blanket or similar piece of material in three inches of mud, he has some idea of the job we had in rolling the camouflage net which is about a hundred foot square, and normally weights about a hundred and fifty pounds. With the water and mud it had collected, it now weighted no less than five hundred. I was in charge of the squad, with the squad leader getting his orders from the Captain; and believe me it was hard to ask those fellows to take hold and lift such a slimey, lifeless, soggy form as that. Finally, however, we succeeded in mounting it on the vehicle, where, to our chagrin, we found that it was about twice its proper size. Through makeshift fastening and a little barbed wire, we finally made it fast, and stepped back to survey our accomplishments. Slowly, and steadily, the inside of the role was slipping out from the pack; like a great snake, it moved until it reached the ground. "Well boys" I said "if we ever want to lose anything, I know where to start. Darn those quarter masters and scientific warfare guys anyway – bunch of rear-echelon boneheads – never been shot at".

Well, our Sgt. finally came back with the "G-2" (army slang for information – intelligence dept.). We were told to prepare to move out immediately. We had placed our 50 caliber anti-aircraft gun on a stationary mount during the night, and had to go some two hundred yards out in the field to bring it in. This was no more accomplished than Lt. John Williams "Long John", our motor officer came up and asked for a runner. His eye fell on me. "McGill" he ordered, "tell the drivers to "turn "em over". My position as Assistant Squad Leader of the First Squad, with rank of Pfc. gave me certain rights and exemptions not granted to the average Pvt., but could I tell the Lt. that? Heck no! So like a good soldier, I trotted off down the road yelling at the top of my voice. "Mount up! Turn "em over! This is it!".

Before the convoy began to move, however, the platoon headquarters track, driven by T/5 Cook, developed motor trouble and would not start. This being the case, our track was next in line so we were to give them a tow. After a muddy wrestle, on my hands and knees, I finally succeeded in making the tow cable fast to our vehicle. This was what our driver liked, any chance to prove the power of his vehicle, or his ability as a driver, was right down his alley. However, his enthusiasm exceeded his ability, and he ended up by sliding into the ditch. By this time the head of the column had begun to move, but the balky half-track was running smoothly...the only trouble was that we were stuck. Our driver was frantic, until he tried backing out, which worked...to his surprise, and soon we were all rolling smoothly down the road – to what – we had no idea.

About noon, we came abruptly around a curve on a steep hill where two "T-2's" (a tank used for repairing damaged tanks – like a wrecker) were trying to pull a swamped tank back onto the road. The tank was halfway down the slope and still right side up, but all the straining and pulling of the other tanks could not budge it.

Up ahead, we could see the M-4 self propelled howitzers of the 493rd Field Artillery, setting out in plain sight on the forward slope of a hill. They were firing frantically at some target we could not see, but the blasts shook the country. I could feel my muscles grow a little tenser and a keen sense of excitement surged through my body. Our vehicles once more picked up speed, as we turned into an open field directly in front but below the artillery positions, the signal came to disperse and dig in. Everyone was glad of that later, because we were all certain that the continued fire of our artillery could not help but draw fire from the enemy. This fire, however, never came.

By now, the rain had ceased and we were beginning to feel a little more comfortable as we dug our fox holes. The exercise felt good, but to our disgust, our holes began filling with water; soon there was an inch and a half in the bottom of each, and still it kept on coming.

The artillery had kept up its firing all this time. With each new burst, the digging men would jump or begin to dive for their holes. Of course when they remembered what it was, they'd grin sheepishly and continue digging. Well, the boys on the big guns up the hill were making so much noise and raising so much smoke, that we figured we could afford to make a little smoke ourselves; so after the vehicle had been covered again, and the 50 caliber machine gun properly mounted and manned, we built a fire from dry potatoe vines which we found near by. In a place like that, small things mean a lot. That fire seemed like all that mattered in the whole world. It reminded us that there still were people in the world who were comfortable and that all life was not this miserable.

Most of the afternoon was spent sitting around the fire, brewing "K" ration coffee and wondering what would happen next. About dusk, the order came down to distribute grenades and ammunition. Each man was to have two pairs of dry socks and be ready to move out on foot. It was an hour before our Squad Leader returned from the C.P. with his dope. He looked serious as he called the squad together and read from his notes as he talked. "We leave our present area at 22 hundred. The squad will be broken into two separate parts. We will meet the third platoon of "B" Company of the 43rd Tank Battalion and proceed from our meeting place mounted on tanks. We don't know for sure where we are going, but we expect enemy artillery fire – in this event, dismount, disperse and dig in. On no account lose the tank to which you are assigned. She's your baby and you are responsible for her. The tankers are counting on you. That's all I have for now, but the platoon will have two guard posts; those not on the guard roster try to sleep. Any questions?".

Of course sleep was out of the question. We busied ourselves by cleaning our weapons inside the blacked out track by the light of a small trouble lamp.

At about 9:30, T/Sgt Huff, of Butte, Montana – our Platoon Sgt. – gave me orders to pull in the outposts. I didn't know where they were exactly, but I wandered around until challenged. It was a great relief to hear someone call "Halt!". I was afraid someone might be just a little nervous and shoot and ask questions later. I gave the orders to disband the post and report to the Platoon C.P. But where our half-track was I didn't know. I was wondering around from vehicle to vehicle trying to locate it in the dark. When I finally stumbled onto Sgt. Huf I tried to let on like I had been looking for him all the time. I was told to join my squad immediately as they were beginning to fall into column for the walk to our rendezvous with the tanks.

The night now was comparatively quiet, with only occasional flashes from shells bursting on the horizon. I don't believe I ever saw such a dark night. The column moved up the hill, the only way I could find my way was by feeling the shoulder of the man in front of me. The mud in the road was sloppy, churned that way by the treads of many tanks. Most of the men had overshoes, but those who didn't already had wet feet.

Presently, the huge dark hulks of tanks rose up in front of us. We counted as we walked along. Numbers thirteen and fourteen had been assigned to our squad. When we finally got mounted up, we found that we were pretty well mixed up, for on our tank was a section of the machine gun squad consisting of Pfc. Szymoniak and Dentino. Those from my own squad were: Chandler, Dow, Drodz and myself. Also from the machine gun section was Edgar "Kid Turk" Turznick of Milwaukee, Wisconsin.

After we had been checked three or four times, someone at the head of the column yelled "turn 'em over". The powerful motors coughed and sputte up and down the line. Soon the night was filled with a deafening cres of nearly fifty tank motors. Sparks began to fly from the exhaust of tank ahead as the power was applied to the treads. Our tank was under way, creeping slowly ahead over the treacherous terrain. In those days, the ground was considered dry when mud only covered your shoes. I had intended to ride on tank number fourteen, as thirteen, according to my suspicions was unlucky. However, fate thwarted my plans and here I was on number thirteen. Later, however, I was glad as number fourteen slid over the bank and dumped the doughboys into the ditch; putting S/Sgt Edwards and Pfc Birtch in the hospital before they'd even fired a shot.

The procession seemed to have moved for about an hour when we came to a halt. It seemed that some of the tanks had become lost from each other. I could hear the radio on the inside of our tank. Someone would give orders to race the motor on each tank as he called by number. Soon everyone was oriented again and once more we were on our way. Before we had gone very far, I fell asleep to the drowsy hum and rocking motion of the monster on which we were riding. It was exciting, but when I'm tired, I believe in sleeping, war or no war, and I did alright.

A light drizzle had started when our column once more came to a halt. It was one in the morning and black as pitch. Sgt. Huff gave the order to post a one man guard on each tank and for the remainder to try and sleep. Two of the fellows found room on the inside, sleeping on the deck plates of the turret; the rest of us were left on the outside to fend for ourselves. As the ground was too muddy for sleeping, to say nothing of walking. The men pulled the tarpaulin from the tank's bedding and equipment rack and we all curled up under it on the back of the vehicle. I had to hang onto a spare boggy wheel to keep from falling off in the mud. Dozing fitfully, I found myself very cramped, cold and uncomfortable. Rather than endure any more of that, I got up and stood leaning on the tank's turret, nodding on my feet. I stood like this for about thirty minutes when I heard a whistling, rushing sound coming toward me and passing in great haste. I waited a second until I saw the flash and heard the crash of the shell as it burst on the opposite side of the hill. Well, the enemy knew we were here at least, but we had out-psychologized him by putting our force on the forward slope; an unorthodox procedure, but alright when it is dark enough. I had left the spot on the top of the tank for the safety of the rear of the vehicle. We had been instructed to crawl under the machine in case of enemy shell-fire, but since it's belly was rubbing on the ground, or mud as it were, there was not much chance of that. However, the eighteen or twenty-four inch deep ruts gave good protection, and I was not too proud to get acquainted with a little more mud. I spent the remainder of the night on guard. The rest of the men seemed comfortable, I saw no reason to disturb them. The only way I could keep warm was by walking back and forth in a tank track which I had found which was comparatively dry. As the morning sun began to send its rays over the horizon, I heard footsteps approaching. After challenging, I found it to be the Company Commander of the tankers. He proceeded to one of the tanks and I could hear him instructing the crew that there was a pill-box out in front which they were to destroy. The tank's motor turned over, coughed two or three times and settled down to a steady roar. I saw the huge hulk plow past in the grey half light of dawn, going out on it's first mission...what happened, I never knew. I listened as long as I could but after it passed over the next ridge the noise was drowned out in the pitter-pat of rain on my helmet.

Someone finally stirred in the tank and the turret opened, a head emerged and someone asked gruffly "How're you doughs getting along?" I tried to sound cheerful when I answered "okay, if it doesn't get any worse than this, we'll make it". Soon we heard the sput and sizzle of the gas stove and a pleasing aroma of hot "C" rations and coffee emerged from the turret. The tankers were getting ready to chow up. I wakened the rest of the squad and with a profusion of gripes and bad language, they emerged from under the tarp and began opening their rations. By this time, the area was pretty well alive with infantry men and tankers getting acquainted with their positions and trying to enjoy cold rations.

The whole forward slope was covered with tanks, as far as we could see. All of course were tactically dispersed, not closer than a hundred feet. When we had finished eating, we started discussing our situation and wondering what was in store for us.

All night occasional sheels had been whistling by overhead and bursting on the far side of the hill with a sound like a door being slammed, but now with daylight, the fire seemed to have ceased. Instead, we could see shells landing on the edge of a wood about two miles from our position. Finally, detonations seemed to be coming from right nearby. To my surprise, almost every clump of brush or grove of trees began belching smoke as the camouflaged howitzers in position put up a withering barrage. Soon a formation of P-47 Thunderbolts came overhead. They circled once, came back in a long line of pairs; the first team peeled off and amid a holocaust of ack-ack, huge and small, came diving at a steep angle on the enemy positions below. We could see the .50 caliber bullets from the planes bounce from the earth and burst in the air as they sprayed the area. The planes disappeared from sight below the hill and soon were seen to rise again on the other side, like kites caught in a sudden updraft of air, they shot into the open sky with tiny black clouds of smoke dotting the air all around them, where shells burst. Suddenly, there was a terrific burst of flame, smoke and fire rolled upwards in a great fireball. The dive bombers had dropped their delayed action jelly-gasoline bombs on their target, and were now safely out of the way of anti-aircraft fire or harmful concussion from the blast which their deadly missile had caused. For several minutes the action was repeated. Two planes going in at a time, their guns blazing, leaving long trails of smoke, as their eight machine guns spat death and destruction on the enemy. Each time too, they would leave their calling card, the jelly bomb, on some hapless tank or Jerry pill-box, the object we could not see. After about an hour of ceaseless pounding from the artillery about our area and from several more formations of planes, the barrage lifted and the last plane disappeared in the West. Now it was time for the doughboys to do their work. Slowly they came from behind a hill to our left which had obscured their positions. The lead scouts out in front, and the main column following steadily behind. Spread out like an army of ants crawling slowly toward some objective. Squad after squad they came, platoon after platoon, with two companies abreast until the hills were covered with men looking like tiny insects.

As the head men rounded the hill, the enemy artillery began it's work. As the first volley fell, the men disappeared from sight. Everyone was flat on the ground, making smaller targets for the flying shell fragments.

These were men of the 29th Division. No green soldiers here. Ever since D-Day, way back in June sometime - it seemed like years ago to us who had only a passive interest in the war at that time - they had been walking, fighting, and dying; from the shores of Omaha beach to the muddy plains of Alsace. It had been the same stubborn, crafty enemy all the way. These men knew what war meant, and they also knew how to fight a war when the going was tough.

When the smoke had lifted and mud all fallen to the ground, the men once more rose to their feet and resumed their march forward. As they moved, shells would drop one by one among their ranks. A man fell to the ground and from where we stood, we could see someone, a buddy or a medic, run over to him. When the column had disappeared over the hill, we could see three or four objects lying on the hillside, some sitting or kneeling, some prone; these were the wounded and the dead. The vicious German "88" had done it's work well, but the American foot soldiers still moved on. Although out of sight, we knew that a battle was raging from the noise which rose.

I felt nausea in my stomach which I had never experienced before. "Oh God" I thought "Why is war? Why do men do these things?". I saw a soldier come back from the other side of the hill. At this distance, I could not tell how badly he was hurt. He seemed to stagger. No doubt he was only slightly wounded but the shock of battle must have hit him. A shell landed only a few feet in front of him, throwing mud and water many feet into the air. The soldier staggered blindly on, like a sleep walker, down into the freshly blown shell crater he stepped and up the other side, as if it was too much trouble to go around. It was only inches that saved him from death. Luckily the shell had passed him as a bursting shell throws most of it's shrapnel forward, thus leaving him in a safe zone.

It had been a big show for us, unseasoned troops that we were. We had grandstand seats to one of the greatest dramas I had ever seen. It seemed much like the operations we had done on maneuvers back in the States. Only this was no sham, this was for keeps, and my mind could not help remembering that those were dead men lying over there on the hillside, and that little group which was gathering were those who still had hopes of living, men who would probably have to face life now without a leg, or an arm. We knew that they were thinking of home and that if another shell didn't find them within an hour, they would be safely on their way back. Way down deep, I guess we all envied the wounded more than we would have liked to admit at the time.

There was not much time to think, however, as a terrific explosion shook the area and mud flew sky high. I could see a cloud of smoke by one of the tanks. My first impression was that someone had fired the tank's 75 mm cannon, but this theory was soon dispelled when I heard the wall of another "88" coming. Of course, it was already past when the sound reached me, but I needed no coaxing to get close to the breast of old mother earth where I lay in a tank track, in a half inch of mud and water afraid to raise my head for fear of getting it shot off by another of those screaming missiles. I looked at my rifle beside me. It was soaked and the muzzle and works filled with mud, dirty, sticky gumbo. I couldn't have used it had I been required to. I sucked the mud from the muzzle with my mouth and rose to my feet. There was a rock pile about fifty feet away and I started for it. On my way, another shell screeched by and I remembered what they had told us back in the States about pieces of rock being as dangerous as shrapnel if hit by a shell. This then was not a good plan so I started back for the tank, only to be discouraged by another shell which put the thought in my head that an object as big as that tank would surely draw fire, so I just dropped right out there in the open, between tank and rock pile. Guess I did my first real praying right there in that rut with shells dropping about a hundred yards long. Finally I made up my mind. I was as safe one place as another, but the rock pile looked safest to me, so I lit out for it. The spot was occupied by two Lieutenants who seemed very pale and rather shaken, but who raised my morale no end by the way they acted, like lions that had been tamed. For once, officers and private were on equal ground. We were all being shot at. Here I was joined by my buddy "Happy" Chandler. He still had his sense of humor with him and it wasn't so hard to smile with him along. I took out my shovel and began to dig; more to be doing something, than for any other reason, as I knew we wouldn't stay here long. Everytime a shell would smack in, I'd drop everything and bury my face in the mud. None, however, seemed to burst very close. We supposed that the enemy gun, or guns, were in such a position that they could not bring their fire to bear on us.

Some more doughboys joined us. They were from "A" Company, they informed us. A very pale and excited soldier came running up with a tattered and riddled pack in his hand. "Don't go over there, that foxhole's no good. They just killed Lassiter and Sgt. _____ is all shot up. They hit my pack - direct hit. It's no good I tell you don't go over there!!". His lower lip trembled and he was the picture of despair. So all these shell were not harmless after all. There would be more along and I wanted to get out.

I was glad when Sgt. Huff gave the order to get our squad together to move out. We assembled on the side of a gully where we worked at throwing the rocks out of a natural depression in the ground. Soon we had quite a crater and although we momentarily expected the company of one of those shells which were zooming overhead, we tried to look and act as cheerful as possible; some chewed on ration biscuits and the rest tried to improve our position or clean their weapons.

"We're moving out!" Sgt. Huff shouted from the top of the bank, "keep your men dispersed and double time". It felt much better to be on the move. When we got up on level ground, we could see the tanks backing as fast as they could go, over the hill. They were going backwards so as to keep the thickest part of their armor toward the enemy and the vulnerable back and sides out of reach.

Our platoon (about 57 men) was strung out along the lip of the gully. Every man was trying to take advantage of the cover afforded by the scrubby, leafless brush which formed more, or less, of a screen. The shells were still falling, but none seemed to come close until we reached the crest of the hill and were descending the other side. You can say what you may about bullets and shells traveling in a straight line, but those "88's" can shoot over a hill anytime they feel like it. The only casualty suffered was Pfc. Luke Gallo who got a chunk of shrapnel through his hand. Pfc. Meyers, of the second squad, had his rifle ruined by another chunk, but did not receive a scratch himself.

Well, it was all pretty exciting and some of it amusing as well as grim. For instance, Sgt. Dow spotted a farm house and had just suggested that we we occupy it when a shell ripped the roof off and sent the chimney tumbling to the ground. That settled that in no uncertain terms.

We must have plowed and slopped half a mile through knee deep mud which had been churned and rechurned by the passing of many tanks, when we came to the abandoned positions of another outfit. Apparently they had been there for some time, at least a day. Their foxholes had ten in one cartons in them for the men to stand on to keep dry.

The ground was littered with broken ration boxes, shelter halves and miscellaneous equipment, but the most revolting was the blood and sickening smell of cordite and Amatol from the shell holes. I'll never forget the feeling of disgust of it all. The outfit had apparently had a kitchen truck there, from the looks of the equipment. It must have received a direct hit and from the blood around, some of it's crew were pretty badly wounded.

Chandler and I picked out a foxhole with only about six inches of water and decided to use it for any emergency. However, I had a premonition against it, so we moved to a different one. It was here that I picked up two extra shelter halves, one for me and one for Frank. Later, they were invaluable in keeping our bedrolls dry.

It was almost dark when the order came to go down into a valley where the rest of the Company and a half-track had assembled, with our bedrolls. "Oh boy" I thought "sleep!" something I hadn't known for about two days. Sure enough, the bedrolls were there and some more rations too.

Out of some ten odd non-coms in the platoon, I was selected Sgt. of the guard this first night at the front. It was quite dark and the men were rolling their bedrolls out on the side of the grass covered hill. I thought it was foolish for all of us to be in one spot, but it turned out alright as no shells hit our area. I was to post one guard at the top of the hill and another at the northern extremity of our area. By the time Sgt. Huff gave me the list of men picked from his duty roser for guard, they were all in their bedrolls and every man looked alike. What a gay old time I had trying to find twenty men out of some sixty bedrolls. If ever a man got cussed more in one night, I'd like to know under what circumstances. I found all but two men and was forced to go back to Sgt. Huff to find out who the next two in line for guard were. I was tempted to forget the guard altogether and crawl into my "sack" like the rest and let come what may, but for some reason, I didn't. I finally got it organized and posted, much to my satisfaction.

I was pretty shaky when I crawled into my blankets that night. I didn't know if my teeth were chattering from the cold or from fright, but they would not stop and I shook from head to toe. My stomach had a hard kn??? and my heart was sick. Those men had died today. I had seen a battle and had been under fire myself. I wondered why none of those shells had not burst near me - like they did for Gallo and Meyers.

No sooner had I started to get warm when I heard the screech of an approaching shell; then the flash and the bank, as it burst on the hill. It didn't take me long to get out and pull my shoes on. If Jerry was going to lay it in here, I wasn't going to be around. However, no more shells came in. I stood and talked to the guard on Sowders half-track the one which had brought our bedrolls. Finally, sleep began creeping up on me and I decided to go back to bed and sleep like the rest. I found it very difficult to stop my shivering, but at last I said to myself that if I was going to die in this war, it might as well be in my sleeping bag. Sweet oblivion finally blotted out my unconsoling thoughts, and I drifted off to blissful slumber.

So ended our first day of combat, on the eve of that memorable day three years ago - December 7, 1941, better known as Pearl Harbor Day.

Note: This record written and soon after the war, in 1948

Chapter II

THE ATTACK

It is almost two years ago since these events took place, and each day the memory becomes dimmer. Not that it seems unreal, but that I try to concentrate on other things. However, at times visions pass before my eyes, and I find myself saying to myself – "Remember how it smelled, Mac? Remember how white those dead men looked? Remember how like pebbles their teeth looked with their lips pulled back in the ugly snarl of death? Remember the bad body odor all the prisoners had, and how they would pass their dead comrades, pretending not to see them? Don't forget it, Mac. You might forget how lucky you were to come out of the war alive and how much you really have to be thankful for. You're a lucky guy!"

Long before dawn the next morning we were wakened from our slumbers and told to roll our sleeping bags in preparation to move out. Sleeping bags were stowed on our single half-track, which immediately pulled up on the road and was gone in the darkness.

The order came to move the men up into another assembly area where the tanks would pick us up. When we arrived in this area, we found fifty or more tanks dispersed about the valley. This was task force "Zebra". We were assigned to tanks of the second platoon "C" Company of the 43rd Tank Battalion. A platoon of tanks includes five vehicles, including the platoon commanders. This, obviously, was a hurry up and wait proposition. By this time it was broad daylight, with a leaden sky and a chilly northeast wind. The rumor got around that "A" Company had attacked the town of Singling with success, and now held a strong position on our flank.

Finally the force on the hillside began to break up. Tanks were disappearing over the hills to either flank. After we had finished a "K" ration, and done a few other front line chores, the order came to mount up, and our little force of five tanks and the first and third rifle squads were under way. As yet we had no organization. We were merely a bunch of men and a bunch of tanks, until the tanks all came to a halt in a low spot.

The tank Lieutenant called for the Infantry officer who was 2nd Lieutenant Willie H. Horell of Bowling Green, Kentucky; a slight, handsome fellow with a little mustache and an innocent looking face. He was about twenty four, I should judge, but there was not a boastful nor overbearing bone in his body. "I'm Lieutenant Hall of "C" Company 43rd Battalion, the tanker said, shaking Lt. Horrell's hand. "I guess I'm to be in command of this force." He was a man of about six feet with hard blue eyes and a wiry build. You could tell he was a man of little fear. After a few more formalities and some chatter he went on "the old man gave me some dope over the radio a minute ago. We are now on the edge of the Maginot Line. We are to attack infantry and armor about this area. The task force is split into many small units like this and we are to work road nets, which means that each unit will follow his particular road until he hits resistance he cannot overcome. We will have radio contact at all times. One doughboy will man the .50 caliber machine gun at all times and the rest will be used as scouts. We leave the L.D. (line of departure) at 11:45. Just then there was a flash overhead and a deafening crash and everyone hit the ground. There was a dense black cloud hanging in the air where the time-shell had exploded. "That's our 105's zeroing in, the Lt. explained. I wondered how many of our boys had been killed by our Howitzers zeroing in.

A strange tank approached and a husky young tank captain alighted. He smiled as he greeted us and seemed to be enjoying the whole thing. Immediately, he began telling of the battle for Singling. He made it sound pretty bad. American and "Heinie" artillery had been firing on our boys with air bursts set to explode about eight feet above the ground. It had been plain murder, he said. This didn't do our morale any good, and neither did the shells which were bursting occasionally over our heads. One of our squad leaders, a man I had respected back in the States, was getting pretty nervous and tried to crawl between the boggy wheels of a tank. His actions were childish and he continually talked about booby traps and mines. His gun was caked with mud and he was swabbing it with a red bandana which he produced from somewhere.

One of the tankers popped his head out of the turret and informed us that someone had just told him that someone had said someone overheard the Germans were about to surrender. This started the talk; soon even conceivable rumor was flying. Someone said Hitler was dead. The path part of it all was that everyone was dead serious, hanging onto the last shred of hope that perhaps we wouldn't have to contact the enemy today.

It was 11:30 and a jack rabbit loped nonchalantly on the scene. Someone cut loose at him with his M-1. The rabbit scurried over the hill unhurt This, however, gave the officers the idea that all weapons should be fired before we moved out, so every gun and machine gun was test-fired.

At 11:40, Lt. Hall gave the order to return to our separate tanks and prepare to move out. As I had my choice of tanks, I chose the Platoon Lieutenants, because, I reasoned, he would stay behind the others to direct them. I was wrong - so wrong - I found out very quickly, for as the force began to move, our tank took its place at the head of the dispersed formation.

"You doughs keep a sharp lookout now and watch out for upstairs window if we pass any houses" Lt. Hall shouted above the roar of the tank. I was lying on my belly on the after part of the vehicle, peering around the side of the turret, my trusty rifle pointed in the general direction of the enemy. Our tank sailed along across the open country like a ship on ocean, it rolled with the contour of the land. The rain soaked sod made a cushion for the monstrous machine and made the ride as smooth as a rocking chair.

Soon the open ground was past and we began to enter more hilly terrain where tanks had churned the soil to mud and the hills were a crazy maze of tank tracks that crossed and criss-crossing each other.

Suddenly, three objects stood out cold and sharp on the hillside. My heart sank as I realized that they were three of our tanks-knocked out. A sick feeling ran through me as I looked at these lifeless hulks with their flame scorched paint and useless cannon pointing in various directions. I wondered how many of the crew members had not escaped these flaming coffins, how many scorched and charred bodies were lying inside those blasted machines.

Our tanks did not stop. On we rolled, past empty shell cases and casings, passed a knocked out enemy 75mm anti-tank gun, with its barrel pointing uselessly at the sky.

Abruptly our tank came to a halt. "Alright, put some Doughs out ahead. I want a thorough visual reconnaissance of the valley ahead", Lt. Hall spoke sharply and I could tell that his nerves were rapidly becoming alert and that he too felt the tension and excitement that we did. Lt. Horell looked hopelessly at Sgt. Dow and the rest of the men. Then his eye fell on me. I tried to crawl into by boots, but could not make myself as small as I felt. "McGill" he said, with his Southern drawl, "you're a good man, go see what's over that hill". Well, I swallowed hard and tried not to think. All at once I knew what it meant to be brave. It simply means being afraid of being thought a coward. As far as I'm concerned I never had a brave inspiration in the whole war. It was either fool-heartedness, or perhaps a little bit of the element of chance, but usually the aforementioned condition that led me to do my duty as required. At any rate, I alighted from the tank and began my cautious way forward. Down the hill I went, expecting at each step to feel the enemies bullet tear through my vitals. As I glanced back over my shoulder, I could see the lead tank crawling slowly over the brow of the hill. The rest of the Infantry was afoot now and Pfc. Drodz had drawn up almost abreast of me. As I neared a patch of brush, bullets began whizzing past my legs and kicking up the dirt in front of me. As I turned my head I could see a stream of tracer bullets coming from the machine gun manned by Chandler. He was giving me wonderful cover, but it was a bit too close for my comfort, so I sidled away from the deadly stream of bullets.

I cannot describe the feelings a soldier has going into battle for his first time. All I know is that I was saying to myself, "if I'm alive this time tomorrow, I'll be awfully lucky". Frankly, I didn't have much hope.

Finally, we emerged from one valley and crossed the hill to the next. As I skirted a small clump of trees, I saw two objects lying upon the ground. At a hundred yards or more, I couldn't make out for sure what they were, but I had my suspicions. As we came closer they began to take shape. There beside a shell hole lay two American soldiers. Both lay on their sides with their helmets nearby, as they had fallen. I felt no sensation of pity, only a regret that our Army had lost two fighting men, but I will never forget how lonesome those two dead soldiers looked lying there on the rain-soaked ground in their rain-soaked overcoats. To this day I cannot look at a soldier wearing an overcoat without thinking of rain-soaked overcoats with dead Infantry men in them, lying in an open field. Nothing can be more cold and clammy than a wet G.I. overcoat. Someone began shooting into the lifeless forms. We had heard so many stories ??? German trickery that we didn't even trust our own dead.

As we cleared the crest of the next hill, the tanks halted and the sco??? came back for orders. Ahead of us were literally hundreds of small pillboxes. They were the outposts of the Maginot Line. "Alright you Dough the Lt. said, the tanks will keep you covered. Any pillbox that gives trouble, just point it out and we will demolish it". That was fine, if only we lived to point it out. The land was as flat as a table and we expected every pillbox to be manned. Carefully I picked my way between the foreboding objects and was surprised that no one fired at me. Drozd and I worked in leap-frog fashion. First, I would get to my feet and about twenty yards while he kept a sharp lookout and fired a few rounds into likely looking openings in the concrete boxes, then I'd hit the dirt and do the same for him while he moved up.

Suddenly, I saw a figure. There was no mistaking it for that of a German soldier. He was running crouched over toward our men on the right flank I thought to myself "Well Mac, it's your first day in combat and you'll about to kill your first Jerry. May God have mercy on you". With that I emptied my clip at the still running overcoat clad figure, but still he kept on going until he was obscured from my sight. I heaved a sigh of relief. At any rate, if I hadn't drawn blood I bet he spent a lot of time in the P.W. Stockade sewing up the holes in his overcoat tail. I didn't have much time to think, as another head appeared from behind the same pillbox and I was exploiting my marksmanship in his direction. Either something hit home, or he got the idea that he could get hurt by sticking his head out, at least the helmet and head disappeared from sight and didn't reappear.

The force moved slowly on to the next hill. Before us lay a wide valley with massive pillboxes on each rise and the hills literally covered with small one and two man concrete emplacements. The tanks on our left were pulling ahead of us fast. Lt. Hall came foreward with his tommy gun to take a look over the brow of the hill. "Something got White!" he told his driver excitedly as he pointed at the lead tank from which was billowing pink colored smoke and flame. No men were visible for some time. Finally, I saw three or four figures walking away from the tank. A hundred yards behind, two more men followed. I learned later that than the tank Sgt. Bill MCBride, the curly headed, smiling boy from Kansas was riding with his boys from the machine gun squad. Later on, he and Lawson were awarded Bronze Stars for that afternoons action. They have activated the tanks fire extinguishing system and helped save the crew.

We didn't have long to watch the proceedings as an uproar on our right flank told us it was time to pull back out of sight. Black smoke was billowing from the area where the artillery shells had fallen among the tank and infantry on our right. Soon the shells were falling all around us and the only protection we could find were the deep ruts left by the tank treads. I spied a large freshly blown shell hole and decided to occupy it. However, I restrained myself for awhile as I could hear another shell rushing at me. "Wham" it burst halfway between me and the inviting shell hole which I had planned to occupy. Well, that was interesting I should have been headed for that shell hole; only three seconds would have made the difference.

As I crawled back, trying to catch up with the tanks, I saw our medic, Pfc. Lynch run over to one of our boys who was writhing on the ground. It was Pfc. Angelo Carucie, the Italian boy who was Captain of the 66th Division championship baseball team. Shrapnel had ripped his leg and arm. The shells were still falling and Lynch, although chalk white with fright stayed out in the open, with the wounded man, administering first aid and morphine. When he had done all he could to make him comfortable, he made a dash for the shelter of our tank. There he began to make out a casualty tag and had the tanker radio back for an ambulance tank, as a wheeled vehicle could never get off the highway in this mud.

Soon we were told to go back up to the crest of the hill to observe. I wiggled my way ahead of the tanks, using a pillbox as a covering shield between me and the enemy. As I got near the pillbox, the tankers settled all my doubts about the emplacement being occupied by sending two high explosive shells slamming into it.

I was glad when I saw Lt. Hall dismount from his tank and with his tommy-gun under his arm wave to one of his tank commanders and shout "come along with me and bring your gun. I want to see if you deserve those stripes!" As the two came abreast of me, they came to their knees and continued on their bellies to a few shrubs which grew on the crest of the hill. Lt. Hall was scanning the terrain with his field glasses, when a shell hit not over ten yards from him, throwing up mud and dirt. The Lt. moved faster than I had ever seen anyone move before. He came rolling like a log back from his observation post. When he was about halfway to me, he regained his composure and stopped. Then he got on his knees again and continued cautiously foreward, back to his old position. Here was a man who talked tough and was tough. I wouldn't have poked my nose over that hill for all the money in the world right then.

Suddenly the roar of tanks and scattered shells bursting was eclipsed by a rushing sound. The knoll on which a great pillbox to our right front sat was suddenly seen to turn black, clouds of dense smoke, dirt and debris shot skyward, as our heavy artillery threw shell after shell onto the pillbox which only a few minutes before had knocked out Lt. White's tank. As the story was told later, the enemy bazooka man had stepped from the door and let loose a deadly "Panzerfaust". The enemy's version of a one shot bazooka. The driver had been killed and both of Lt. White's legs broken. The men riding on the rear of the tank pulled the external releases of the fire extinguishers and proceeded, under the direction of Sgt. Wm. McBride to extricate the wounded and shocked tankers. Sgt. McBride and Pfc. Lawson later received Bronze Stars for this action. They were working under small arms fire from the pillbox near by.

Barrage followed barrage until the entire hill was pock-marked like a giant cheese and the concrete walls of the fortress were chipped and broken.

The tank behind which I had been squatting began to move again. With my squad well dispersed, we moved forward. Sgt. Dow had received an accidental wound in his foot which left me in charge of the squad. It was bad enough going under fire for the first time, but now I had nine other men to look after.

Something ripped overhead with a sound like cloth tearing and I saw the firey tail of a tracer shell not over a foot above the buttoned up turr of our tank. For some reason, the Infantry was told to hold their positions while the tanks went forward. Chandler and another man started to walk back when I saw a blinding flash on the turret of the tank, not fifteen yards from Frank's head. I saw his helmet fly and both arms and legs spread out. "Oh, oh" I thought "there goes

Happy". I was feeling pretty blue when up came Happy, smiling as usual with a dry crack, expressing his thoughts about people who bounce 88's off tank turrets when Doughboys are around. I was really glad to see him in one piece. According to him, he didn't even know the shell came close.

The tanks disappeared over the hill and we were told to pull back over the crest and dig in. We didn't have to be told twice. Chandler and I found a large size shell hole and crawled in. After about ten minutes of hard work, we had it sufficiently enlarged so that we could sit on the bottom with our legs beside each other. "No use of being eager about this" my companion remarked, "nothing can get us now". He began to op??? a "K" ration, but before he got the top off, the high scream of an .88 interrupted his operations. As we buried our faces in the mud, I only had time to pray "Oh God" before the shell burst. I didn't have time to say "not this time". Happy slowly raised his head, and with an earnest look on his face, quietly picked up his shovel and began to dig. No sooner did we cease digging and begin to open our rations than another screaming missile came over our heads. The digging began immediately. This went on all afternoon. Each time the shells burst, we would begin digging until dusk began to fall and we emerged from our holes to find Lt. Horrel and Sgt. Huff had gone off with our tanker to have a little sport hunting tiger tanks.

S/Sgt. Fisher was in charge of the platoon. He gave Drodz and myself orders to try to locate Lt. Horrel. We walked to the top of the hill and then we did a very foolish thing; something we had been told over and over not to do. We began to shout "Lt. Horrel, Lt. Horrel". No answer for a second and then the sky was dotted with hundreds of burs of 20 mm anti–aircraft shells. They weren't within two hundred yards of us, but it told us one thing, that it wouldn't be smart to call again so we retreated with all possible haste to where our buddies awaited in a draw.

After trudging along down the hill for a half mile or so, we came to a medium sized pillbox in the bank of a dry ravine. Into this we all filed, leaving one man to post guard. At last! we could remove our equipment and relax. The pillbox had been abandoned for sometime, it was obvious – probably had never been used. It had rather large openings for doors and windows. Disregarding this, many of the men began lighting cigarettes. The light from their matches clearly lit up the room and must have shown out plainly through the windows. Someone cussed, told them where they could go. The men were in a nasty mood and the strain and cold was beginning to tell on them. Many were getting swollen feet from being cold and wet – the first stages of trench foot. As yet, my feet were dry but the tips of my fingers were quite numb and felt cold.

By and by, I heard the sound of tank motors. The vehicles were creeping stealthily along the road toward our position. I shuttered to think what it would be like for an 88 to come slamming into this room filled with men. I felt no little anxiety until someone announced that they were friendly tanks and would spend the night nearby.

I must have fallen asleep there on the damp, cold cement with only my raincoat for covering and my grenade pouch and canteen for a pillow. When I awoke, it was gray light and some of the men who were lucky enough to still have some "K" rations left, began to nibble at them. Neither Happy nor I had anything but a few biscuits left, so we contented ourselves with them.

Before much time had elapsed, Pfc. Bratcher came running up with orders for us to join Lt. Horrell at a bank about half a mile north of us. When we finally succeeded in gaining the top of the hill, on which we met our platoon leader, we felt very much enlivened and warmed by the exercise. What was better, the tank had a whole case of "k" rations which soon became quite empty. The whole platoon tried to find a place to ride on the massive monster.

We rode for about two miles, some of the men trailing behind, as the one tank could not afford enough handholds for us all. Finally, we came to the remainder of our force, setting sedately on a hillside, all eating rations and making coffee with the heat from the little gas stoves which the tanks carried.

The tankers were relating stories of the great battle they had at dusk the night before. There, ahead of us in the hollow, was grim proof of it's reality. A monstrous, rusty, burned out Tiger tank with one tread shot away and it's eighteen foot 88 drooping sickly toward the ground. According to the talk, our tankers had bagged four such prizes, with no loss to themselves. Sgt. Huff related how he had spotted one of them behind a pillbox by seeing the light tan colored gas can tied to one side. The Jerries always carried their reserve fuel supply in these five gallon cans which were painted light tan since the African campaign. These cans stood out well and really made a fine target.

This third day seems like a blank to me. I can think of no train of events between morning and nightfall which could recall our action that day. I do, however, recall later on that evening now we walked over to the burned out tank. The atmosphere about the whole thing was gruesome. As I think of it now I don't see why it should be, but I remember the smell of the burned flesh and the ammunition. The empty shell cases and the cracked and crumbling plastercoat on the sides and the turret of this dead thing. There were personal letters scattered around the vehicle...letters in German from some poor home frau to her husband who as an Ober Lieutenant in this particular Panzer Outfit. It made me sick to think and imagine this wife's sad face when she heard of her man's death. Right there, I made up my mind that I would have to keep an open mind - not to think about anything and above all forget what I saw. That was the only way, as far as I could see, to ever keep my nerves from going completely to pieces.

That night, a half-track came up with our bedrolls. After the usual confusion of selecting our own, we finally got straightened around. Myself, Chandler and Drodz were picked to go with Pfc. Best to man an outpost in a pillbox on our left flank. When we got there, we found that a reconnaissance outfit had beaten us to the sleeping space, so we were forced to roll our beds in the small room where the former garrison had kept it's coal. It had also been used as a latrine, as we soon found out much to our disgust and we all went into our sacks express our opinions of the living habits of certain German soldiers we'd like to know.

My turn for guard never did come, for at four o'clock, I was awakened from my uncomfortable slumber and told to roll my sleeping bag as we were preparing for a daylight attack. We were to jump off inside of an hour. It was pitch dark, both inside and out as we did our best to roll our bedding on top of the pile of coal. There was muffled profanity and talking as we moved between the sleeping reconnaissance men, on our way to the door. We came to the conclusion that they had not appreciated the presence of guests in their abode. At least not guests who arose early. When we emerged, we were surprised to find the ground covered with four inches of soggy, wet snow. Tucking our rolls under our arms, we made our way toward the tanks where Sgt. Huff and the rest were waiting. We were divided into groups again and assigned to separate tanks.

Soon we had to be reassigned, as the tank to which we had been directed bogged down and couldn't be budged.

"As soon as the situation becomes definite on our right flank" St. Huff said, "we will jump off, better eat if you can and change socks if possible. Weiner and Kahn had to be sent back with trench foot yesterday. I don't want to lose any more men". We also learned that Nick Martin, one of our mortar men, had been badly wounded the day before and was on his way back.

I was shivering, I was cold, I was homesick and above all, I was scared God had seen fit to spare me thus far, but then He had spared most of the men. Sometime my turn would come and I knew it as sure as I breath.

The dawn broke and nothing happened. Chandler, Drodz and I went on a little scouting expedition down over the hill. There, standing across road was another giant Tiger tank, with the muzzle of its 88 pointed directly at our tanks. We immediately hit the ground in the slushy snow which was just beginning to melt. "Run and get a bazooka" I told Drodz "and tell them we've found a tank". The vehicle was so still we knew no one could have seen us, so we crawled closer, trying to keep the crossroad between us and the tank so that we wouldn't be seen. We watched the silent machine for sometime, waiting for Drodz to return. We became discouraged and made a break back over the hill to the tanks. We were angered to find Drodz talking calmly to a group about the tank. "That tank's knocked out, you guys" he informed us, "they got it yesterday". Well, I was much relieved that I didn't have to become a hero yet, but I thought one of those tanks would have made a nice souvenir.

The attack did not come off as was planned and the men stood around in the slushy snow discussing the situation and nibbling on "K" rations. Two tanks had bogged down and some of the men had to be switched to other vehicles. Sgt. Scott was evacuated with appendicitis.

As the sun rose, that is as the grey dawn broke, I was assigned to outpost duty to guard against a surprise attack. I took my post boldly in front of an American tank which had both of it's tracks blown off by mines. A boggy wheel had been blown off with such force that a telephone pole had been sheered off completely. Earphones, helmets and other crew equipment were strewn about the tank, in the mud.

As I stood meditating on these grim evidences of combat, a low flying L-5 artillery observation plane came winging overhead. It was immediately caught in a hail of ack-ack. The flimsy ship dived steeply to escape the rain of death which was bursting all about it.

For about an hour, I watched the plane fly back and forth, trying to spot the offending gun position but with no avail. While engrossed in this pastime, a very ordinary looking G.I. came strolling down the road from the direction of the pillbox about two hundred yards up the hill. He looked very ordinary to me and I addressed him as "Mac". He seemed very cool and collected, but my manner of familiarity changed suddenly when I saw the gold leaf of a Major's insignia showing from under the mud on his helmet. My "Mac" immediately changed to "sir" and I couldn't use it often enough. I realized I was talking to Major Novesol of the 43rd Tank Battalion.

As we stood discussing the observation plane, a burst of ack-ack dotted the sky quite close to us. We realized that we'd been spotted and drew back immediately to the welcome shelter of the tank. By this time, the L-5 pilot had called on another plane to help him knock out Jerry's "A-A" gun. As the number one pilot climbed directly into the field of fire, number two flew low over the approximate location of the gun. But, Jerry was smart and the air was surprisingly still; not a shot was fired and the planes gave up in disgust and went winging off over the hill to find new targets. I imagine there were a few Heinie anti-aircraft men who felt plenty relieved to see them go. Having 155 and 105's landing in your lap isn't exactly what makes for a pleasant morning's diversion.

As I walked back up the hill toward the pillbox, I could see small figures working their way up a big hill about two miles distant. Before them, our artillery was laying down a devastating "rolling barrage" which is wave after wave of high explosive shells bursting only a hundred yards or so in front of our troops. This has a tremendous demoralizing effect on the enemy as he doesn't dare to poke his head from his foxhole long enough to take a pot-shot. It also inflicts a lot of casualties in our ranks, if not adjusted just right. As the figures moved up the hill, puffs of smoke could be seen rising as enemy shells lit in their midst. It was a gruesome sight, but from this distance, a rather intriguing show to watch.

"We're moving out, Mac" Huff informed me "better go back to your tank. When we cross the railroad below the hill, the Infantry will dismount as those wires overhead may be alive and the rails will make too good a ground; someone might get electrocuted. The town on our right has not been taken yet, but we are to pass that. Keep a sharp lookout in that direction. By the way, Juan and Casey were wounded, also Nick Martin. I think we'll get relieved tonight though".

As our tanks rolled over the hill, about fifty strong, we made quite a spectacle, spread out as we were, all over the terrain. I thought to myself "what a foolish thing to do, now we're right out where they can see us". I guess I thought we'd stay in hiding for the rest of the war.

Suddenly the .75 mm guns on the tanks started to crack and the force came to a standstill. I could see shells bursting in a small brick switch shack by the side of the railroad. Evidently someone had spotted a sniper or some movement. At any rate it was only a matter of seconds before the building was completely demolished and we were once more on our way forward. The doughboys were on foot, as the lead tanks were crossing the rails. Once across, we once more mounted up and went rolling along over the soggy terrain, crashing through barbed wire fences as if they were non-existent.

More gigantic pillboxes lay ahead and the enemy held town was plainly visible on our right. A few scattered shells were bursting, but as yet no ill affects. The force held up on the side of the hill and the dough boys dismounted and moved up to one of the pillboxes on foot. As for myself, I took two men and took up positions behind some waste concrete and rocks with our rifles covering the town. The artillery was coming in quite fast now and the tanks had moved on up the slope, leaving the Infantry crowded around the pillbox. Several had climbed down into the moat which was designed to protect the lower entrances from attack. It would have been a terrible catastrophe had the enemy concentrated high artillery on the pillbox at this particular instant. One of the laws b??? which an Infantry outfit lives when in combat, is not to get in a bunch but to always be dispersed to avoid too many casualties from one shell.

Lt. Horrell gave the order to move on up the hill to the next pillbox. Someone had tried the door on this one and it had blown up inside. No doubt it had been booby trapped, but either the wiring was faulty or the charge not big enough, as no damage resulted. As we passed through the tanks, I looked over a hedge into the wide shallow valley beyond. A highway ran between two large pillboxes which stood on the crest of the hill. The countryside beyond was in flames. To our immediate left front, a town burned and smoked, while still more phosphorous and high explosive shells burst and flared up. At least five or six towns were visible, all of them in flame. A feeling of hopelessness prevaded my being as I gazed on these towns and the smoldering smoke filled valley. This was a cruel, hard war and people were dying over there by the dozens. I didn't have long to reminisce however, as a barrage of artillery came crashing in. Once more, I crawled and groveled close to the breast of old mother earth, which at this time was wet and sticky with ankle deep gumgo and more mist falling. I saw a water–filled foxhole and made up my mind then and there that I'd take my chances on top of the ground rather than get any wetter by throwing myself into one of those unspeakably obnoxious holes. Shells were bursting all about our tanks. Great black clouds of smoke rolled after each barrage and mud flew sky-high. My clothes were soaked clear to my chest and stiff with Alsace clay. I was miserable and cold. Lt. Horrell was now on his feet moving among his men with cheery words, but it didn't take much imagination to see that he was feeling mighty low and discouraged himself. As I rose to my feet, I saw an object which looked like a flaming match come floating through the air. Instinctively, I stuck out my left hand to try and catch it. Good thing I didn't, for as the missile snapped by waist high, I realized it was a tracer bullet. It still had plenty of zip left to have torn through anyone's guts who may have gotten in front of it.

The tank guns began firing furiously and as I watched, I saw the flaming tail of one .75 mm shell hit an object and bounce into the air. I was surprised when I realized that I was looking right at a gigantic Tiger tank. The first live one I had ever seen, but it wasn't a welcome sight.

Suddenly, all of our tanks began to back up. Some of them turned tail and pulled out as fast as possible. The order had come down to withdraw as it was getting dark and the terrain was not fit for night fighting with the tanks. It was with thankful hearts and many a backward glance that we mounted our tank and went sailing back to the pillbox about two miles away, from whence we had jumped off earlier in the afternoon.

When we arrived at the pillbox, the lead tanks were already forming a defensive perimeter so that they could spend the night with their backs to each other so to speak and their guns pointed in all directions.

We proceeded to the pillbox where we found a field artillery outfit setting up its O.P. (observation post) in the cast iron turret. The medics were also looking the place over for a favorable aid station.

Soon the chilly, shivering doughboys had fires started and "K" ration coffee a brewing. Well, all I had was a few dry biscuits and I was too cold and miserable to eat anyway. My bare fingertips were numb and swollen. Chandler complained that his feet felt numb.

For the past four days I'd been willing to give anything I owned for a pair of gloves. However, I was lucky, I had overshoes and my feet were dry and warm. Now, two years later, when I think of the boys who were evacuated that night with trench foot and trench hand, it still makes me angry with the rear echelon troops, living in warm billets and wearing the shoe packs and overshoes that could as well been on the feet of one of our boys. Bobby Kahn lost two toes because of it. Sam Weiner and S/Sgt. Fischer had to be evacuated with trench foot and several others who I don't recall; not to forget Chandler whose feet were swollen and blue and so big that he couldn't get his shoes back on.

Happy and I found a pile of straw in a corner of a drafty room and proceeded to pile it over us. It felt good to get our equipment off again, but the bodily weariness was so great that even food didn't appeal to us. We curled up in each other's arms like two children trying to keep each other's wet body warm with our combined efforts.

There beneath our pile of straw, we found warmth and sleep slowly creep over us. I was awakened by the sound of men moving about and flashlights flickering. "Come on" Mac said "the outfit's moving out; we've been relieved by the 2nd and A.T. Platoons!" No sweeter words had ever reached my ears. It took little coaxing to get us into our suspenders and rifle belts. As I started to leave the room, Chandler discovered that his feet pained him so that when he walked, he was unable to navigate. Someone called a medic who informed us that a jeep was about to leave for the hospital in the rear and that Happy should be evacuated. I hated to see him go, but felt just a little envious as I thought of clean sheets and real American girl nurses. This left only myself and Pfc. Drodz, of the original nine squad members, who would be coming off the line this night. Birtch, Gangard and Ell, I learned later, came up with the relief element.

As we trudged down the slushy road to the rear, my heart was thankful that I was still a live mortal and able to breathe. I think I must have breathed a little prayer of thanks to my Maker as we slogged along.

A group of Infantrymen who have been without proper sleep and food for a week or so are a pretty hard bunch of fellows to get along with. The slightest remark may cause your best friend to say things he doesn't mean. The men feel like talking when they come back. They don't brag but they do not appreciate anyone who may claim to have done more hero deeds than the other. Then too, everyone has a different story to tell about any one incident and this usually stirs up harsh words. However these feelings and arguments last only a few minutes and then all is forgotten.

After some little difficulty, we located our Company's vehicles biviouaced in a broad defile, well dispersed and camouflaged.

"There will be hot coffee in the kitchen" someone announced as we broke ranks and stumbled to our squad vehicle. The hot coffee held no attraction for me tonight. All I wanted was dry underwear and my sleeping bag. Sigmund Ryfinski was overjoyed to see us and I really believe he showed some emotion other than selfish, grasping ego which was his usual manner. "I look after my boys" he boasted as he pumped up the miniature gas stove and began brewing coffee. I was busy stripping off my wet, soggy clothes and digging dry, clean ones from my seat cover. The vehicle had been blacked out and we had the electric trouble light burning. It was very cozy and warm to sit cross-legged and barefooted in my soft, clean, dry G.I. long underwear. It was one of the most luxurious moments of my life. Sitting with a cup of hot coffee in my hands and with the sounds of bursting shells so far in the background that they sounded like the roll of thunder was very comforting.

It was only a matter of a few minutes before I was comfortably settled in my sleeping bag, drifting off to the coma-like slumber which only a physically and emotionally exhausted person can experience.

When I awoke, I could hear voices and the rattle of mess kits, as the men who had already risen hurried toward the kitchen truck and a warm breakfast. It was still very dark in the half-track and I thought twice before I left the comfort of my sleeping bag to look out on the cold, drizzly world which was the rolling plain of Alsace.

The kitchen crew was in an exceptionally fine mood this morning and fed the men dehydrated eggs mixed with bacon, as long as the boys kept coming. It was good to see them again too; Sam Davis, Stemple, cheerful little Gafeney and even Mess Sgt. Ohla. The scrambled eggs even tasted good this morning after almost a week of field rations.

My biggest thrill came when I saw an Army truck, a six by six came rolling down the sloppy road, past our bivouac and on toward the front. Yesterday, or the day before, we had fought for that road. Yes, two days ago the German army was running up and down this highway, but now, thanks to our boys, it was an artery feeding our front line. Trucks could even travel it alone, without a convoy or any other protection.

The stories and rumors were flying as we stood around and ate, using the fender of a nearby half-track as a table. The best story though was about the 2nd Platoon, under Lt. Hune, "The Goon" which had blundered into a little town which was in the process of being captured by an American outfit. Before they realized what was going on and stopped the convoy, a sniper cut loose and put a bullet through the radiator of T/S Filas's half-track. The situation might have been serious, but as it was it turned out quite humorous. However, when some of the fellows realized they were being shot at, they cut loose on the first thing they saw move and one of them shot a civilian which wasn't to our credit, but I guess it was a pretty good shot anyway.

The day was spent in cleaning weapons and napping and just enjoying being alive. Although the sounds of war were still present, they were so far in the background that we had put them out of our minds.

About three that afternoon, Sgt. Huff announced that Bettweiler had fallen and that we were to move in and hold the town.

Just before dark we reached the outskirts on the west edge of town. To my surprise, it was just over the hill from the pillbox where our tanks had been held up the day before. The town was still smoking and one barn was throwing a reddish smudge into the sky, giving an eerie air to an eerie situation. We dismounted and carried our bedrolls into town afoot. The vehicles were not to enter the town as yet as artillery was still bursting on the far edge of the village.

It was easy to find a house to billit the platoon in, as all the civilians were gone. There was a gapping hole in the roof of the kitchen of the apartment that we chose. I decided to bunk with the machine gun squad, so Drodz and I found a room with a bed and began to make preparations for supper and sleep.

The bed felt wonderful that night and although shells burst quite close during our slumber, we saw no need to hit for the basement as the sleep was more inviting than dodging shells.

In the morning, we were awakened by the deafening roar of bursting shells. It took no more invitation for us to depart for the "Kellar". There we found company, namely McBride and Marino. The desire for safety was soon forgotten in the fervent hunt for canned food and souvenirs. We succeeded in finding several bottles of sweet fruit juice and preserves. The lady of the house must have thrown up her hands in horror when she saw the numerous bottles and glass jars which had been opened and partially emptied.

We soon learned that our kitchen crew had moved in during the night and hot chow was to be served. When we emerged into the fresh air, we were surprised to see a greenish looking projectile with fins on the tail, partially buried in the street, directly below our window. During the night, a dud mortor shell had fallen and thank God, didn't go off. We made sure to make a wide detour of the unwelcome piece of ordinance.

The civilians were coming into evidence now, from cellars with sand-bagged windows and heavily timbered doors. They looked pale, tired and dirty and their gaze was not exactly what you'd call friendly.

The day was comparatively uneventful, but we stayed near our house with the cellar door ever handy. A tank crew was living on the ground floor with their vehicle parked directly in front of the door, it's cannon pointing down the road by which we had entered the town.

That evening we were placed in an old barn on the south edge of town, covering a road which led to the next enemy village. During the night we stood guard in pairs. The straw on the barn floor was very welcome and we slept well, despite the fact that Jerry seemed to know we were there. Every fifteen minutes, or so, three or four shells would burst so close that dirt would come raining down on the roof. The outpost detail was under the charge of S/Sgt. Sabin of the Mortar Squad. Morning was quite welcome and we rolled our bedrolls and moved back to the town.

After breakfast, McBride and I went back to the road which we had been guarding during the night, in search of a dead German which someone had said was lying by the road. We found him, lying in the gutter, face down, an olive green bundle of soggy overcoat and wool uniform. He was blonde, with wavy hair and I should judge about 25 years of age. Well, we felt that the sooner we got used to looking on death, the better off we'd be. As we rolled him over with our feet, we saw that jeeps and other vehicles had been running over his feet and that now they were mere pulp in the black hob-nailed shoes which were fastened to legs which were limp as rags because the bones were in a million pieces. His face on one side was covered with the dark brown manure water which was flowing slowly down the gutter. It was an ugly face, with a mean twist to the mouth and a long nose.

Beside him lay an American billfold with several small notes in English. Some unfortunate doughboy had been looted by this character only a day or two before. Now the irony of war was beginning to make itself evident to us - perhaps tomorrow a German soldier would stand over my body, examining my souvenirs and my ravaged carcass.

"There's another in the shed over there" a passing soldier informed us. We moved over to the large machine shed, which he had indicated, past a civilian man and woman who looked at us with unmasked hate and uttered some words which sounded more like oaths to us than conversation. There on a flatbed of a wagon, lay the blue clad body of a Jerry artillery man. The top half of his torso was nude with only a medic's bandage covering the gaping hole high on the right side of his chest. The greenish hue of his skin against the dark bed of the wagon gave him a gruesome air and I felt I had seen enough for the day. I was glad on one score at least - not all of those devils had escaped the fire of our rifle men.

The next month passed swiftly, with no action except patrols for our Company. There were showers in Saltzburg, a few days of billeting in Barondorf, Christmas and New Year's in Rohrbach, where we felt very grateful for the fact that we didn't have to spend the cold days on the line.

On Christmas Day, Chandler returned to us from the hospital. He was a sight for sore eyes and it was good to have him back. Kitchen, Happy, myself and Pfc. Russell from the 2nd Squad decided to take a walk in search of souvenirs. We ended up by going into a gigantic pillbox - down, down, down, the stairs wound until we wondered if we'd ever reach the bottom. This was the Maginot line of which we had all heard so much. All the light we had was the cardboard from a ten-in-one case which gave off a yellowish, smoky flame but which, nevertheless, was sufficient for our purpose. On the bottom of the shaft, we found corridors leading into barracks, wash rooms and officers quarters. The plumbing was intact and we could even get cold water from the tap on the wash basin.

The urge to explore became too strong and we wondered off down the first corridor which looked like it led someplace. With cardboard almost expended, we came to a "Y" in the tunnel. It didn't take long to make up our minds to stick to our own path. There was a breeze of wind coming to us now and we walked faster and faster as our fuel supply rapidly depleted.

To our unspoken relief, we came, finally, to a stairway. It was an exact duplicate of the one by which we had descended into the tunnel. As we emerged from the bowels of the earth, we saw a faint glimmer of light. The roar of an artillery piece reverberated through the concrete structure, with a hollow sounding echo and re-echo down into the far reaches of the radial network of tunnels. To the best of our knowledge that was an American gun, but it could have well been an enemy piece, firing from the cover afforded by the massive pillbox.

I rushed to the small porthole through which the light of the overcast winter day was filtering and blinked at the sudden change from dark to light. The hole through which I was peering was designed fro a gun port and was too small to afford a portal of exit. Looking around for a way out, we were quite alarmed to find no visible means of exit. It was an effort to stave off the feeling of being trapped and lost with the sun shining rapidly in the west. The rooms in the fortification seemed to have been used as a repair depot for automatic and anti-tank weapons, judging from the many pieces of ordinance and replacement parts. Many of the guns were of French make and had, no doubt, been there since the German forces had taken over three years before.

I climbed into the cast-iron turret and looked out the small machine gun ports onto the surrounding country. Slowly, the realization came back to me, as I made out familiar landmarks. It was the same hill from which had been driven two weeks before, by the appearance of a few Tiger tanks..

The novelty of hunting souvenirs and rummaging in the various drawers chests made us forget that we, as yet, didn't know how we were going to get out. Our spirits, however, rose to a new high when Chandler picked an empty "K" ration box. A "G.I." had been here before us, so there maybe a way out.

"Here's a new stairway" Kitchen informed us. It was so well concealed behind a door that we hadn't noticed it till now. Lighting a bunch of straw for light and also the cardboard ration box, we followed Kitch down two flights of stairs and to a small opening in the wall. At last! Freedom! Words cannot express the relief we felt upon being in the open again. The only way out of the moat we found ourselves in, was to climb up a steel pipe used for a conduit of some sort. As Chandler started I came suddenly to the realization that I was weaponless. Had I left my rifle in the other pillbox or dropped it somewhere along the way? Hot blood rushed to my face and neck as anxiety crept over me. A soldier without a rifle was in a mighty bad spot. But how far would we have to go before we found the piece? Well, all I could do was try, I came to the conclusion. So - back in we went, hardly expecting to find it. We were back on the second floor when I spied it leaning on a chest of drawers. I grabbed it like a long lost friend, and I'm not sure but what I could have kissed it. Old faithful had traveled with me all the way from Texas, to England, and had made it in good shape all the way to the muddy plains of Alsace, in excellent working order. She had seldom been over ten feet from me for the last four months, except when I went to London or Salzburg on "pass".

When we emerged again from the pillbox and climbed up the pipe, we began to wonder where Russel had gone. We spied a pillbox about a quarter of a mile south of us and set out for it. When we arrived, we saw Russel heading over a hill into town. A few shouts and whistles brought him back. His amazement was amusing. He didn't quite understand how we could have gone down one hole and come up another.

The tabacco-chewing Pfc. from Kentucky had been inspecting some French weapons when our little exploring party set off and hence had been left behind.

While we stood talking near the pillbox, a man hailed us from a passing jeep. He wanted to know where a certain artillery battery was. Apparently he thought we were from that outfit. He stopped his jeep and came walking over. On his belt hung a much coveted "P-38", a genuine German pistol. I think the first thing I said to him was "Let's see what you've got there, Mac". I had been talking quite informally for quite awhile until I asked him what his outfit was. "I'm C.O. of "A" battery of the 403rd Artillery Battalion; that floored me for a second. The man looked like any other G.I. to me, but I finally realized that I was talking to an officer. From then on, I couldn't "Sir" him enough to make up for calling him "Mac".

When we reached town that evening, the men were straggling up the street to the kitchen. It didn't take long for us to get our mess-gear together and fall in line. There was turkey and all the trimmings... cranberries and candy. I ate my supper sitting on a wagon tongue with my mess-gear setting on an abandoned pile of Jerries' artillery shells. Needless to say, I enjoyed it immensely. The outdoor life had given me such an appetite that I very seldom could resist going through the chow line for the second time, but the fresh food was so different from the dry concentrated food to which I had been accustomed for the past few weeks, that my insides turned to water and I developed a very unpleasant case of dysentery which made my nights a series of cat-naps. In that cold weather, with no sanitary facilities, it was very uncomfortable.

New Year's Eve, I was Sgt. of the guard. After the roster had been arranged and all the men notified, I sat down to write a letter home. As I sat composing and thinking very little about things about me, a shot rang out and everyone in the room jumped and turned white in the pale candlelight.

I guess I felt I had to set an example for the man, as I grabbed my helmet and rifle, and was on the way to the door, before the echo died away.

Frankly, I expected to be met by a hail of lead as I emerged, but everything seemed perfectly still and quiet. I walked up the street and met S/Sgt. Juan and a few of the boys from my squad. They were all quite steeped in the fumes of schnapps. They all claimed to have fired the shot and when the First Sgt. showed up, Juan insisted that he had done it. Of course we knew he hadn't but we let it pass as a mere New Year's celebration and who were we to prevent a few of the boys from letting off steam.

The Herrlisheim area is where we met the Tenth SS Panzer Division head on on January 16th 1945 The Twelfth Armored Division is credited with blocking another major German Army breakthrough, at a terrible cost. We were only on the line four days, but sustained staggering losses in men and equipment.

Chapter III

DEBACLE AT HERRLISHEIM

It was the night of January fifteenth, nineteen hundred forty-five. The gray winters day had given way to an even grayer evening, when a runner arrived from the Company Commander. "All non-coms are to report to the C. P. immediately." He didn't stick around to make small talk, but hurried down the stairs and out into the darkness from which he had come.

I threw another stick or two of wood into the old brooder stove that we had "liberated" and were using to heat the small attic room that we had called home for the last week or so. I didn't have to bother with putting on my field jacket or my little wool cap as the temperature of the room seldom reached above the freezing mark and these items of apparel helped to make the place more liveable. I donned my rifle belt with suspenders, gathered my rifle and helmet and went clamping down the creaky stairway, following my squad-leader, S/Sgt. Don Juan.

As we moved hastily down the stairs, Sgt. Juan threw his head back toward me and muttered some unsavory remarks about officers who insisted on having cadre meetings at the very moment when we were getting settled for the night.

The company C. P. was in a "Gasthouse," or tavern, directly across the street from our erstwhile billet. As we entered the large dining room/bar-room, we noticed that all windows had blackout curtains and that the walls of the room itself was attractively covered with dark wood paneling, which in normal times would have been considered sumptuous. Now the dimly lit room was filling with the non-coms and officers from each of the four platoons. People were shuffling about, talking in low tones and the air was filled with cigarette smoke. The thud of rifle and carbine butts was heard, as they were being stacked against the wall, tables and chairs that filled the room. The crowd began to quiet down.

Judging from the expressions on the faces of Captain Powers and the other officers, we knew instinctively that this was not to be just another problem.

"At ease men." It was Captain Powers speaking. "We have just been alerted to move out. Have all your vehicles loaded and prepared to leave by twenty-one hundred. We will go by vehicle to the town of Hoerdt, there we will dismount and proceed on foot. We will be with Combat Command "A", under General Ennis. Your platoon commander will give you further information. Be sure each man has ammunition, dry socks, and rations for two or three days. Carry on." With that he turned and joined a discussion with other officers behind him.

We followed Lt. Horrel to a separate room, where he spread a map out on a table, and very seriously began to explain the situation. "There are about two hundred German infantry dug in in this area in front of a woods. The woods is about four kilometers from the town of Hoerdt, and five kilometers from the town of Whitting. The French hold the town of Gambsheim on our right flank and will jump off at four to occupy the town of Offendorf. Offendorf is about three kilometers from Gambsheim. "A" and "C" companies will be in the assault and will jump off at 0400. "B" company, that's us, will be in reserve. There is reported to be about six tanks in the area, so be sure to take all of your bazookas and plenty of ammunition. Here, and here are machine gun positions reported by a reconnaissance patrol. We will probably knock them out with combat patrols. They are primarily outposts. The main line of resistance is about two hundred yards closer to the woods, but within rifle range. Each man will be issued material with which they are to make camouflage suits. See that each man does this in the best manner possible. That'll be all. Have your vehicles lined up at ten minutes to ten. Sgt. Huff has the camouflage material." With this he rolled up the map and went back to the main room.

As we climbed the stairs back to our drafty smoky room, several of the fellows, seated on their bed rolls, were writing letters. They demanded to know what the score was. "Looks like we're really in for it this time, guys." I replied. "We have to take some woods with about two hundred Jerries all dug in just waiting for us to walk up so they can make fodder of us." It wasn't a very inspiring speech on my part, but I felt that it might make the boys realize how serious the situation really was. It was over a month since our initial introduction to combat and the time had been spent in Seventh Army reserve, patrolling and training. At one point, the Battle of the Bulge had almost required that we go north and participate. As things worked out, our presence in the Strassborg area was even more urgent. Actually, some of our units had been alerted and were on their way to Belgium when this need caused them to be recalled. It looked like we were about to have a "Bulge" of our own.

The long weeks without contact with the enemy had resulted in some restlessness among the troops. Some were getting pretty cocky, thinking that the war was nearly over and that we were somehow special and not likely to be called on for bitter fighting.

Enter, Sgt. Huff. He stuck his head in the door and tossed in a roll of cheese cloth. "I don't know any more about how to make a camouflage suit than you do, so suit yourselves as to how you make them. Only be sure that you are well covered. You'll stand out like a sore thumb if you don't." With that he closed the door and turned and proceeded down the stairs.

By nine o'clock we had our half-track loaded and in line. There was much hurrying and bustle, not to mention the usual confusion. At last we were off. I took my place beside Sgt. Juan the gun turret. It was spitting snow and quite cold. The brisk wind was blowing snow in our faces put our gloved hands over our mouths and noses to keep them from freezing.

As our convoy rolled slowly past the war scarred old church on the hill, we could see, in the darkness, the hulk of the burned out Sherman tank still sitting in the gate of the high stone fence that surrounded the church and cemetery. We never dreamt that we would ever see the town again. What different bunch of soldiers came back five days later!

The boggy wheels played a steady stucatto over the hum of the exhaust, as we rolled steadily along. I thought of the tank back at the church with the shell hole in the turret. It looked like a hot knife had been poked through a slab of butter. I also thought of the hip-bone, that I had seen, lying in the front seat. This was all that remained of the burnt body of one of the crew. The fate of the rest was not known.

We passed a little shrine, with crucifix, on edge of town. The convoy soon stopped at a road intersection, waiting for the rest of the battalion to take it's position in line. On our left, laying sickly it's side in the ditch was another brute of a tank. Another Sherman. The gun turret was blown away and now lay in the field about twenty feet from the blasted hull.

In the past few days we had covered this territory on patrol and had pretty well scouted all the surrounding fields and woods. I thought of the body of a Luftwaffe officer that we had found, lying in woods off to our left flank. His corpse was frozen and his head was earless. I wondered if some revengeful doughboy, or some partisan had removed the ears as an indication of a mission fulfilled, or in reparation for the brutalities he and his family had experienced at the hand of the enemy in days past.

Again, the column was moving and I took a seat between the driver and my squad leader on the warm steel deck. The muffled voices of the men in the rear, and the hum of the motor made me a bit drowsy, but the tension was building and sleep was the furthest thing from my mind. On and on we drove. I relieved Sgt. Juan on the gun and strained my eyes over the unfamiliar countryside, trying to spot any suspicious movements by the enemy and ever on the alert for signals from the car commander in the vehicle ahead. Only the red "cats eyes" and the shadowy outline of the next half-track with it's commander protruding from it were visible.

Finally we rattled into the outskirts of a town and the column stopped. It seemed like a fairly large town. As we waited in our vehicle, two French soldiers approached out of the darkness with a loudly protesting woman. One of the men wore the band of the cross of Lorraine on his arm. This was the known symbol of the F. F. I., or the Free French underground. "Kesker c'est?" I asked. "Nazi," was the reply. "Avez vous un cigarette?" After cigarettes and hand shakes were exchanged, the soldiers moved on, escorting their still uncooperative guest.

"Dismount your men and get your snow suits on." It was the husky whisper of Sgt. Huff. "Keep your men at ease and no lights. Disperse and wait for orders." The white camouflage suits came out of the packs and soon we were a silent writhing group of ghoulish figures trying to get into the hastily contrived and crudely made snow suits. Of course the column began to move before we were well into them and confusion reigned. A profusion of muted oaths filled the air as the still struggling doughboys squirmed and tugged at the awkward coverings There was bazookas and bazooka ammunition to be looked after. Each man had at least four grenades and an ample supply of rifle ammunition. In addition to this, we were required to carry the ever present gasmask. All in all, we looked like a spooky pack train as we headed for the outskirts of the town.

As we slogged down the street, Sgt. Huff stood on the curb and checked each man as we passed. I had decided that freedom of movement was more important than not being seen and had cut holes in the camouflage material for my arms. It took a lot of "fenegeling" to get comfortable and also to have most of ones body covered.

As the column halted again, a barrage of artillery lit at the edge of town off on our left flank. So there really is a war on after all. The men all up and down the column heaved a sigh and sat down silently huddling close to the buildings and fences. Directly across the street from us was another silent white clad column. The Second platoon. There was a creak of equipment and a clang of rifle butts on frozen ground or curbing, as the men got to their feet once more, and the husky word was passed down. "Let's go."

We emerged into the country on a well traveled highway. Things were relatively quiet and as we passed the hastily thrown up roadblock of wagons and farm equipment, the thought of home came to me. This was January 16th, my mother's birthday. What a fine birthday gift it would be if she were to get a telegram about me before the day was done. Right then I made up my mind to do all in my power to stay alive just through that one day. The rest would take care of themselves.

It was a bit difficult to keep the men from talking and most of all from throwing away their grenades and bazooka shells which were cumbersome and hard to manage. This was unforgivable conduct and many of them lived to regret it. The equipment we carried and our heavy winter clothing made the march difficult but there was no excuse for leaving their entrenching tools in the half-track as many of the men did, much to their later dismay.

We passed over a railroad viaduct and observed many pieces of rolling stock sitting motionless, covered with the new fallen snow. The country into which we emerged was still and white. There seemed to be a tension in the air and that old shivery feeling was with me again. I didn't know if it was from the cold or fear. My jaw was tense and every muscle in my body taught. Of course my thoughts were not very consoling as I was expecting the worst.

We turned off the road into a large field, which seemed to me, although it was covered with snow and ice, to be prairie. Here the signal to halt was passed back and we all got silently down.

The order to put outposts on our flanks was given and I took two men off into the murky lackness till we could barely see the figures of the rest of the company laying prone on the ice.

The gray fingers of dawn were creeping out of the east when we returned to the main body. As we came near the rest of the company, a rushing sound reached our ears and we hit the dirt, or rather the ice. With a crash and a bang, smoke and flame, the shells landed about three or four hundred yards to our left. It was then that I saw the figures of running men silhouetted against the shell bursts. Another and another salvo crashed in, but still the men continued to run. It was the boys from "A" company. The attack was on and I sent up a silent prayer of thanks that I had been lucky enough to be in "B" company, the one that was to be the reserve element.

It wasn't long before small arms fire began to crackle and the sound of two or three viscous sounding machine guns ripped off their song of death. They played the old tune. One on the left, then the one on the right and then one from some other sector, setting up their deadly cross fire through which nothing could pass standing up.

It was emotionally worse for us, I believe, lying back there on the ice, imagining what was going on up there, than it would have been had we been included in the attack.

Gene Tierney, of the mortar squad, was laying bellydown not over ten yards away, when a spent bullet came sizzling over head. I looked up just long enough to catch a faint hint of a grin on his tense face.

Up ahead, we could see a six-by-six truck with a crew of men working with some bulky objects. I learned soon that they were the Nineteenth Engineers, and the bulky objects were parts of a foot bridge on which we would cross a canal.

It was quite light now and Sgt. Huff came walking back from where he had been surveying the situation. We could see the front of the column moving. One and two men at a time would dash across the bridge and disappear over the edge of the far canal bank. "Keep low and get across as fast as you can,"

Sgt. Huff ordered. "The first squad will be in front. After you cross, move down the canal a ways and deploy your men as skirmishers." Somehow, I found myself leading the platoon as soon as the footbridge was passed. To tell the truth, I didn't know just what to do, so I merely pushed down the canal and took up a position facing the direction from which the noise of battle was coming. All I could see from where I lay, was the smoke of the bursting shells on the edge of the woods. Our artillery was getting some good tree bursts. They looked good from where we were.

We held these positions all forenoon, while the heavy mortar squad from Headquarters company set up on the back side of the canal and lobed their shells over our heads.

As we sat on the bank of the ditch alongside the canal, in which the entire company was disposed, a shell came whizzing over and clipped the branches from a tree above my head. Apparently, the force of the branches was not great enough to detonate the shell, or else the shell itself was a dud. It did not explode. If it had, no doubt a lot of us would not have lived to tell about it. Although the troops were not close together, a tree burst has a much wider range of dispersion than a shell bursting at ground level. Tree bursts are very effective against troops that are poorly entrenched.

It was about four in the afternoon, when a line of widely dispersed infantry came slowly from the direction of the woods which they had attacked early in the morning. There was only a few at first, but they kept coming until there was fifty, or more. We watched as they would hit the ground as they were fired on. They would spring to their feet and run crouched over and zig-zagging to spoil the aim of their adversaries.

I was busily digging my foxhole, when the lead man from "C" company came up. He looked mighty tired and worn. We didn't know what they had been through in front of the Steinwald Woods that day. All of the men following looked the same. From their appearances they could have been in the line for a week. They looked unshaven and dirty. Most of them had shed their white camouflage suits.

There was Pfc. Toy, whom I had known back at New Mexico A&M, Sgt. Hugonon, and several more officers and men with who I was familiar. "Where is the rest of the company?" I asked one of the doughs. "They're still up there," he answered, "dead." That last word hit like a thunderbolt. Massive numbers of dead had never occurred to me. These were men, some of which I knew. I had been in ASTP with several of them, and we had all trained together at Camp Barkely. I felt disheartened and sick. All that had seemed worth living for had disappeared. Hope that I had for living through the war now seemed very small. I realized that this was a small incident in a global war, and that it probably wouldn't even get a short column in the papers back in the States. Even though it was all important to me now, the only thing that really mattered was that I was still alive and that I could still hope to see my home again. It was about this time that I heard the most nerve wracking sound I had heard so far in the war. It was a screech like a shell glancing off the turret of a tank or a pill-box. I also likened it to the sound of a dog being abused. When the sound came again and again from the direction of the woods, I decided that it was nothing that I knew anything about. I learned later that this was the German Army's Neblewerfer, or rocket gun. (Some called it the "Screaming Meme") The fact that I didn't know what made the sound was most depressing.

Long after the main body of retreating infantrymen had disappeared in the trees along the canal, there continued to be stragglers. They made their halting way from the trees, which obscured their battleground, to edge of the canal where we were entrenched. All had the haggard and worn look of men who had been thru a literal hell for the last eight hours.

The non-coms were called to the C.P. and the "dope" given out. "A" and "C" companies had met up with stiff resistance, now it was time for "B" to go in. The plan was for us to go up with a company of tanks. Elaborate plans were made, as to the disposition of each squad after we had completed the first and second phases of the attack. As I proceeded back to my squad, I spied Sgt. Bill McBride busily digging in his light machine–gun. I could tell that he was as worried as I was. In a weak and somewhat vain attempt to say something that might cheer us up, I shouted, "Hey Mac, I wonder what the price of little green apples is in Kansas City today." With a half hearted and somewhat displeased smile he replied dryly, "I don't know, but I sure wish I was there right now."

Well, the attack never came off. Somehow or other the orders were rescinded. I suspect that Lt. Col. Clayton Wells, our battalion commander, having lost two of his three infantry companies in the attack, that day, was not about to commit his sole remaining company into what could very easily mean the loss of his entire fighting force. I'm sure he had a hard time convincing his superior officers that this was not the way to win this part of our war.

Information came down that the French had also met with failure in their attempt to secure Offendorf, the town behind the woods. Our flank would now be seriously exposed if we did, indeed go through with plans to reattack the woods.

So far, our company had sustained only one casualty. Pfc. Looser, an old army man who had seen action in the Philippines. He had been nicked by a chunk of shrapnel and started back on foot for the aid station, when another mortar barrage caught him squarely and riddled his body with shell fragments.

I had dug a sort of makeshift combination foxhole and slit trench in the bank of the ditch and was trying to get some sleep. The residuals of "A" and "C" companies had dug in directly behind us on the higher bank of the canal. As night closed in I had the satisfaction of knowing that I had lived through another day. News came that the kitchen truck was coming up as soon as it was dark. Of course this brought our moral up a hundred percent. Instead of the truck, as promised, all that showed up was a couple of half-tracks, driven by T–5 Ryfinski and T–5 Arbuckle. They had hot coffee, doughnuts and bed rolls. Much to our pleasure, they also brought mail. What could we do with a letter out here where no lights were allowed? I had two letters. One from Grace and one from Mom. I knew who they were from by the glimpse I got when sorting them out inside of the blacked out half-track.

Getting back to our foxholes in the dark, was not an easy proposition. I was in charge of a bunch who insisted that I was leading them in the wrong direction. I maintained that I was right and although I didn't come out where I anticipated, I did find the squad again and handed out the doughnuts and mail to the hungry doughs. Kid Bratcher had a box, from home, of cookies which lasted roughly two minutes. Believe me, we really appreciated each other families when they sent things like that.

I don't remember how we got through that night. All I know is that we were moved back across the canal at about three o'clock that morning. The company lined up and were served hot coffee, right out there under Jerries nose. Funny that they didn't smell the stuff. G. I. coffee has a awful strong smell.

Finally the company began lining up in a long column. The word was passed around that we were to go up and hit the woods again. It was too early in the morning to become very excited, but the suspense of standing around waiting to shove off was terrible. We must have waited for at least an hour before the head of the column began to move silently ahead. It was a relief to be moving, even if we didn't know what lay ahead. Most of us still had on our camouflage suits. Fresh snow had fallen during the night and a few flakes were still floating down, giving the world around us a surrealistic mood.

Things were terribly quiet as we marched silently across the canal foot bridge once more. Only the squeak of the snow under foot and the creak of our equipment broke the silence. There had been a faint red glow on the sky for some time, in the direction of the woods, and as we approached to the south, we could see the outline of a tank. Red flame and smoke was boiling from the tanks turret and the bogey wheels were aflame. As yet we did not know it it was one of ours or one of the enemies. As we came closer we could see that it was a Sherman. Sparks and flame would fly at regular intervals as the heat became too great for the ammunition stored inside. There was the fast crackle as a string of machine gun cartridges went off, and then a violent explosion as a cannon shell would explode. I wondered how many of our comrades were still inside that flaming hull, their bodies being slowly cremated by the flames.

The column stopped just outside the range of the light which the flaming tank gave off. I'm sure that the enemy had, by now, obtained an accurate picture of what was about to happen, and that our numbers and position were well known.

Orders to get down, were given, and we all "hit the dirt". In this case snow. Word was circulated that the point had hit a mine field and that the engineers were now trying to breach it. I managed to get separated from my squad somehow and when we had hit the dirt, I found that I was with the second platoon instead of the third where I belonged. I wondered about for some time and had just located my squad, when the ominous sound of an incoming mortar barrage reached us. Whoom! Whoom! Whoom! The shells were landing too close for comfort. We knew that it was no coincidence that they were landing so close. We had been spotted beyond a doubt, and now Jerry was trying to spoil our plan before we got a chance to put it into action. Our supporting tanks were now coming up in our rear and with the noise they made, were also drawing some fire. When the first shell hit, I was on the ground with my fingers biting into the frozen dirt. As the second and third barrage smacked in, I could tell that they were getting farther away. I became drowsy and almost dozed off, laying out there on the snow covered prairie, with mortar shells landing less that one hundred yards away. My sleep was hindered, however, by the whisper of a shell that was too close to be meant for anyone but me, or some of my buddies. I had time to pray before it hit. I don't know what I said, but imagine it was my usual prayer when things were breaking fast. "Oh Lord, not this time." Then it hit. Frozen chunks of dirt and ice came raining down on my back and shoulders. The concussion of the explosions made my pants legs billow as if a strong wind was blowing. My head throbbed from the sudden pressure change. That first shell was followed by another and another. All of them were so close that each time they hit small bits of ice and dirt came raining down. The barrage must have lasted twenty minutes, and when it finally lifted we had only one casualty, a man whose name I have forgotten, who had joined us about two weeks previous, as a replacement in the mortar squad. He had only been in the army about four months, and had been sent directly to Europe from his basic training camp without so much as a furlough. I remember him as a quiet man, of about twenty-five, married with two or three children. We never did get well acquainted. The only thing I remember about him was that one night when I had him on my guard roster, he was sitting cross legged on his bed-roll, writting to his wife when I came to get him. It was his first chance to write home since he left the States and now I had interupted him by putting him on guard. I suppose his widow got the letter after he was dead.

The shells were falling behind us now, in the area where we could hear our supporting tanks moving up.

The order was given to withdraw. Several casualties had been sustained by the lead elements in our formation, including our artillery observer, Lt Arbuckle. I was the last man in the column, so assumed it was my duty to lead the retreat. (A responsibility that I was more than glad to take.) I almost made the biggest mistake of my life, heading straight for the sound of our friendly tanks. Before I knew it, I was right in the midst of the tanks and a furious mortar barrage. I saw a mortar shell hit on the turret of the tank beside me. The commander was standing in turret with the top half of his body exposed as he directed his driver. A shell exploded directly in front of him. In my mind, I still see him, silhouetted against the light of the explosion. His arms were raised and his body slightly bent at his waist as if to counter the force of the blast and the accompanying shrapnel. I wanted desperately to get out of here. Engineers which were now being used as Infantry, were in support of the tanks and following them on foot. As I was trying to escape the situation, another shell burst nearby and I watched as a man went down. He tried to get up, only to fall helplessly back to earth, sobbing, "I'm hit! I'm hit! My leg!" A buddy rushed over to him to give what help he could.

I'm out of here! My squad, which had dutifully followed me, was still with me. Thank God, the rest of the company had sense enough to not follow into that holocaust. We rejoined the main body just as they were about to cross the canal on a bridge that we had used in our approach earlier in the morning. We crossed, one man at a time, bent low and running at top speed. There was still the possibility that Jerry would try to knock out the bridge to cut off our retreat. I'm sure that he was so pleased with the results of his shelling, that he decided to leave well enough alone. At least he didn't shell the bridge as we expected.

Our column headed back up the canal to the area from which we had jumped off about three hours earlier. It was light now, and I was anticipating a chance to read the letters I had received the night before. We passed a bogged down Sherman tank, with only the turret and one corner of the hull now protruding from the frozen quagmire in which it had sunk a few days earlier. It was a helpless looking brute with it's seventy-five mm. cannon pointing uslessly at the sky.

The morning passed swiftly, as we all were anticipating, yet dreading the next move. About ten o'clock we ??? out again and met our half-tracks in a defalated area. We were glad to see something familiar that moved on ???. We were tired of walking.

Lt. Horrell gave us the dope on the attack that we were now ordered to make. The plan was to have the ??? ride the half-tracks until fired on, then dismount and enter the Stainwald Forest on foot. The column of ??? began to move, and soon we were rolling smoothly down a road which seemed to be taking us in a great ??? movement of the targeted woods. Apparently our orders had been changed, and we never moved into the ??? forest.

After about an hour, we arrived at what I presumed was the southwest flank of the woods that we had tried to ??? morning. It must not have been the same woods, however, as our vehicles stayed out in plain sight of the and not a shot was fired at us. It had me very confused.

The area in which we were now, showed definite signs of battle. There were two bogged down Sherman, and one light tank which had broken through the ice in a swampy area. Also, there were piles of O. D. overcoats and other equipment, which another outfit had she to make them less encumbered for the attack. The saplings and brush all around had signs of machine-gun fire. Much of it had been cut off about waist high and what was left standing had nicks from multitudes of speeding bullets.

To our surprise, and pleasure, we were allowed to wonder freely about the area. We assisted the crew of a tank recovery vehicle in stretching out the cable from the winch on the wrecker and hooking it to one of the tanks that had gone through the ice. The disabled tank, however was stuck beyond the power of the salvage vehicle to move, and the non-com in charge was forced to give up temporarily, while he radioed for additional help.

We walked freely around the area, without paying any attention to the possibility that we were being observed by the enemy which, in all probability, was still defending the woods. It seems now, as I look back at it, that the whole move was a feint, that we were merely put out here to cause the enemy to shift his forces to recon with us.

We stumbled into an abandoned enemy observation post which had been captured by our forces during the preceding battle. It was very cleverly hidden inside a large hollow tree, from which the back side had been removed by fire and decay. Footholds had been chiseled from the firm wood, which allowed the observer to climb six or seven feet up and peer, undetected though the profusion of branches that spread out at that height. Beneath the tree, were foxholes for at least four men. In these we found all their gear. Rifles, "Panzerfaust's," grenades, shaving kits, tooth brushes and even boot polish. Two or three bayonets were found, which some of our men took for souvenirs, as was our habit whenever enemy equipment was found. The troops rarely carried them for more than half a day before they were deemed to be too cumbersome and got rid of them.

We also found some foul smelling cheese, which I had to taste to satisfy my curiosity. This cheese was very attractively wrapped in tinfoil. When I bit into it, I was reminded of the Alsace farmyards with their front yard manure piles. I spit it out immediately, but I'm sure my breath reeked of it for hours afterward.

One of the foxholes was a well built dugout, with branches, covered with a blanket and a thick layer of dirt for a roof. There was room inside to comfortably sleep at least two. The floor was covered with straw. As I entered on my hands and knees, the thought of booby-traps entered my mind. The spirit of adventure, and by curiosity soon overcame any qualms I may have had for personal safety, and I proceeded to explore.

About dusk, we all assembled around our half-track. Someone started a fire and we all heated water in our canteen cups for "K" ration coffee. Knawing on the hard biscuits, eating the other contents of the "K" ration, and drinking hot coffee tasted good. After we had all eaten we began to feel the joy of living again and to realize that life might not be all danger and discomfort. It's in times like these that the men start speculating on what is going on back home. The feeling that we are forgotten is bound to come up before the session is over. Someone will express his sentiments toward "4-F ers," and what they would like to do if they could get their hands on one right now. Someone will make a funny about what post war life will be like in a veterans home. Fantasies of little ones lined up in ranks for inspection each morning, and the G. I. language that might be used in after war life, is always good for a laugh or two.

As soon as it started to get dark, the order came to "Mount up." We were all glad to be on the move again after a weird day. Noone seemed to know where we were going as the vehicles pulled out of the area in a well dispersed column. We rattled easily along the trail being made by the lead half-track. Eventually, we picked up T/Sgt. Eblem from our anti-tank platoon. He ordered us to hold up until the rest of the company caught up. Somewhere along the line we had become separated from the main body.

By this time, many of the men in the back section of the vehicle were dozing off. The warmth of their closely packed bodies, the hum of the motor and the lack of imminent danger all worked to enhance relaxation and eventually slumber.

When the column began rolling again, Sgt. Eblem clung to the side of the lead vehicle and directed the driver down the trail that we were to follow. Our course took us parallel to a canal until we came to a fairly open area where trees and brush no longer obscured our vision. Up ahead, we could see the burning, flaming buildings of what appeared to be a fairly large town. This was our first view of Herrlisheim. After our vehicles stopped, Sgt. Huff came back with the information that the town was held by our forces, and that we were to enter and take over from Combat Command "B".

After a long wait, during which nothing happened, our convoy was formed into a circle with the noses of our half-tracks and those of a tank company, which had joined us, facing outwards. We must have looked much like the early settlers did with their covered wagons, when in Indian country.

Against the purple and red tinted clouds of smoke rolling from the inflamed town, I could make out the gutted skeleton of a church steeple and what seemed to me to be the forms of running men. Whether it was actually men or just the shadows from the flames, I wasn't sure. At any rate it was ghastly and it gave me a sense of insecurity. No one seemed to know just exactly what the situation was at that moment.

We worked out a guard roster, and those who didn't have to go on immediately found places alongside the vehicles, where they unrolled their bedrolls, and sought the secure feeling that only a warm bedroll can offer.

My tour of guard duty did not come till two in the morning, but I was not the least bit tired even though it had been a long and somewhat tedious day. I strolled over to the side of the canal where a column of out 119th Engineers were waiting for their orders to enter the town. They were tired and hungry. We shared our rations with them, much to their appreciation. They had been acting as infantry for the last two days and had had it even tougher than we.

As I stood and conversed with some of the engineers, three shadowy figures approached along the canal bank. The long dark coats of the men in front were unmistakably those of German soldiers. As they approached, we could see that they had their hands on their heads in the usual sign of surrender. Behind the Germans, came an American soldier, herding them along, with his rifle at high port, ready for use, should any of his prisoners decide that he didn't like the idea of being a POW. "Colonel Evans sent me back with these" the guard informed the engineer platoon T/Sgt. "Said you were to take care of them." "What are we supposed to do with them?" someone asked. "I'm going to shoot the _____ right now and get it over with." stormed the platoon Sgt. pulling up his carbine. To this such a volume of dissenting voices arose that he lowered the gun and looked around. "I'll do it, you guys don't have to watch if you don't want to." I stepped forward, and a little timidly informed him that I'd take personal charge of the prisoners and guard them myself, rather than see them killed in cold blood. To this there was approval from the men standing around the Sgt. "Okay, I won't shoot them," he promised. Turning to one of his non-coms, he ordered, "Put a guard on these men." With that he turned and walked away, leaving the junior non-com to take care of the guard detail.

As I was about to turn in for the night, I saw a sheet of flame in the area where several of our tanks were parked. The shells began to fall thick and heavy in this area. I was about to run for cover, but decided that the spot I was in was as safe as any. A high round passed overhead and burst across the canal. All became still again.

There was intermittent shell fire all through the night, but I finally fell off to a coma-like sleep. When I was rudely shaken into wakefulness for my time to go on guard, it was still very dark, but the names of violet smoke still rose from the burning town. I made my way to a tank on the outer perimeter of our defenses where the guard I was to relieve was standing. "Halt," the guard demanded. "Give the password." I complied and after a few words of conversation, he retired. Now I'm alone, except for the sleeping crew inside the tank by which I stood. I moved about carefully, just to keep warm, until another barrage of mortar shells fell too close for comfort. I hit the dirt and listened as more shells continued to fall. I became worried about the safety of my sleeping buddies, and ran back to where they lay and woke most of them. No one seemed to realize the danger they were in and many of them expressed their displeasure at being awakened.

As the shelling ceased, I made my way back to my guard post. I took my position farther away from the spot where the last barrage had fallen, and on the opposite side of the tank. I stood motionless and silent, as I imagined moving figures out there in the empty night. I finally got hold of myself and made myself realize that if this kept up I'd soon lose my nerve. In the silence which followed, I could hear the rumble of several vehicles. Far off, over a slight hill, I could hear a prime mover, a truck, or perhaps it was a tank. The engine was snorting and racing, apparently trying to get into position. Someone honked a horn and a loud voice shouted. It reminded me of the noises we used to hear back on the farm in North Dakota, when we were kids. We could hear the neighbors, about a mile away, just completing their evening chores, as they shouted and moved their noisy livestock from one area to another. But this wasn't North Dakota and the sounds we heard were not those made by a domestic family. This was Alsace, and the sounds came from the throats and the war machines of a bitter and ruthless enemy.

It was four o'clock when my relief came. As yet there was no sign of dawn. There was no use for me to try to get more sleep, so I wondered back to the canal where one of the engineers was guarding the prisoners. Sometime, during the preceding hours, another prisoner had joined them, so now there was three. There they were, on their hands and knees on the ice. They had not been allowed to lie down all night. The only positions they had been allowed to take were standing, kneeling or on hands and knees. At all times, they were required to keep their hands in view of their guard. I felt very little pity for them, mostly thinking how lucky they were to be alive and out of the fighting. I knew that the fate of many of us would not be as good as they now had it.

The heavy pungent body odor wafted to my nostrils. It reminded me so much of dead Krauts that I turned my back and strode back to our vehicle, where I began to roll up my bedroll.

By the time I finished the housekeeping task of rolling my bedroll and eating a breakfast "K" ration, the area was awake with men on their knees rolling their own bed rolls and talking in subdued tones.

The stillness of the morning was broken by a quick succession of shots. I knew at once what was up and started out at a trot for the area where the prisoners had been kept. As I came close to the small knot of men I could hear some one shouting in a terrified tone. "No! No! No!" Then another quick succession of shots and all was silent. My heart sort of did a summersalt and my stomach knotted. I turned around and headed dazedly back to our half-track, without staying to view the bodies. I was thinking of the "Frau und svie Kinder," which one of the prisoners had told me about the previous evening. I heard three louder blasts from a rifle, as the engineer Sgt. administered the "Coup de Grace." I was informed later by Chandler, who had seen the whole thing, that the same Sgt. who had threatened to kill the prisoners the night before, had received his orders to move out. What to do with the prisoners? This was his big problem. Without making any "bones" about it, he stepped up and emptied his carbine into the three men. When this was done, he took a rifle from one of his men and finished them off. According to Chandler, someone then asked the Sgt. how it felt. "Feels swell," he replied, "wish I had a hundred of them. I'd shoot every _____ one of them."

Our company moved across the frozen canal on foot, leaving our vehicles which were to return to the rear areas. The line of march took us in the direction of the still smoldering town of Herrlisheim. We followed the canal until we came to a small creek that ran at right angles. The creek, of course, was frozen, but the shallow banks offered a small degree of protection from view from the town, and of course from rounds fired by snipers. Our mission, according to Captain Powers, was to enter Herrlisheim and rescue the remnants of the 56th Armored Infantry Battalion. This, however, seemed to be as far as we would be going for now, as all communication with the surrounded troops had been lost. As the assistant squad leader of my squad, I ended up on the extreme left of the company skirmish line.

It was light now. The frosty haze of the dawn was lifting, revealing the town, directly ahead, about five hundred yards away. On either side of the outskirt buildings were large pillboxes, one was about two hundred yards from my present position.

As I began to prepare my "horizontal" foxhole, by digging into the bank at a level even with the ice on the creek, I became aware that several of my men had neglected to bring their entrenching tools. Now they were anxiously waiting for me to finish digging so that they could use mine. As soon as I had dug far enough into the bank, that my head and body would be protected, I gave up my tool. To my dissatisfaction, my legs and feet still were exposed, lying out on the ice. Since the topsoil was frozen to a depth of about six inches, I had been able to tunnel far enough that my head was completely covered. I felt somewhat like an ostrich seeking safety by burying it's head in the sand. I went into a nearby cornfield and came back with an armful of stalks, which I placed carefully in the bottom of my new home. I was about to crawl into my shelter when the crack of a bullet let me know that we were now under fire. It didn't take long for me to get down, but most of my men, as yet, had very little protection. Pfc Kuter, of Fon-du-Lac, Wisconsin, now had my entrenching tool, and began to dig like a mole. A few more sniper bullets smacked the air about us and the situation was no longer was funny.

About this time, a small group of G. I.'s came walking and running from the town. The word soon got around that CC-B had been completely killed or captured, except for a few stragglers. One of the men who told how he had really been having a time escaping the enemy, sported a wicked looking Lugar pistol in a massive leather holster hung from his belt. Around his neck hung a pair of German artillery spotters glasses, the barrels of which must have been ten inches long. After allowing us to handle and admire his trophies, he assumed the prone position and began to scan the buildings at the edge of town with the spotters glasses. After a bit, he laid his rifle on the ground before him and took careful aim. To our surprise, he fired a series of tracer bullets into an upstairs window of one of the houses. This was very disturbing to me, as I knew that none of our troops were ever issued tracer ammunition unless it was interspersed with other rounds in a machine-gun belt. I suppose that snipers might have had some, but the ordinary infantryman did not. I rationalized that this fellow had been shot at so many times during the last few hours that he had lost all caution, and with the lust for blood that he had attained during the bloody fight the night before, had thrown all caution to the winds. After firing a clip of tracers at what he told us were German soldiers in an upstairs window, he began to appear to get a little nervous and took off on his hands and knees for the rear. When the first mortar shells began to fall in our area, I realized that we had probably inadvertently helped one of "theirs" to spot and betray our position to their mortarmen.

As I lay there, I got the surprise of my life, when I saw what I had taken for granted to be a patch of snow at the base of a utility pole, get up and walk nonchalantly away. Since the snow that had fallen the day before, had now melted, except for a few spots where it had piled up in drifts, we had shed our white camouflage outfits. Not so, the Germans. Their suits were much more permanent than ours, and they, no doubt, had no choice but to wear what they had on. I was certain that this was no American soldier. Resting my M-1 on the frozen ground in front of me, I took careful aim. Making adequate allowance for distance and for the slight northerly wind, I slowly squeezed the trigger. To my surprise, the white clad figure dropped to the ground and lay motionless. When I looked again, an hour or two later, it was still there. No one came to his aid or to move him. If, indeed, I did hit him, it was purely a lucky shot.

"Stop that shooting!" Captain Powers thundered at me, "don't you know that our boys are in that town?" Maybe they were, but it wasn't any of our men that were trying to set up the machine-gun which we knocked out with mortar fire a few minutes later.

As we lay there, waiting for something to happen, a Jeep drove up with hot coffee and oranges for the engineer company which was digging in on our right front. They had a few extra oranges, and out of the warmness of their hearts, they threw out enough for each of us. We threw caution to the wind and for a few minutes men were dashing back and forth in full view of the town, retrieving the fruit. We had been trained not to expose ourselves like this. It was something that had been drilled into us day after day, in training, and with the experience that we had had so far, we should have known better.

I was laying flat in my foxhole when the first mortar shell came over. It lit about fifty yards long. This was the signal for the Jeep to depart, and depart he did. With a roar, and a cloud of dirt and dust, he left at top speed. He literally tore out of there. Someone dryly remarked that this could not be enemy fire, but that it must be our own artillery trying to zero in on the town. That theory was soon disproved. It didn't make any difference to me if it was ours or theirs. I planned to stick in my trench. I was really glad I did, when a full blown barrage came slamming in. I was flat on my face with my head in the hole that I had provided for it. The ground shook, and so did I. Our visitor with his tracer bullets had done a remarkable job, and the innocent American soldiers had unknowingly helped him.

No more shells fell for some time, and I observed the figures of two men moving boldly down the bank of the canal in our direction. They came within easy rifle range. I took for granted that it was some more of our boys coming out of the town. Suddenly, they must have been surprised to see out positions so close, they made a dive for the ditch and disappeared from sight. Apparently, the Germans were closer to us than we realized. I'm sure that the two enemy soldiers were surprised as well, to see us sitting right there under their noses.

Only minutes after this, the shells began to fall again. This time it was one murderous barrage after another. Now they were falling short of our ditch and landing in the field in front of us. I was glad that my dugout had been made big enough for me to stretch out, but me feet seemed terribly big out there on the ice. The barrage didn't lift for one second, but they all fell so short that I was inclined to think that it actually was our own artillery and that they were trying to protect us from an enemy counter attack. I was hoping that this was true, until a barrage lit too close to carry any illusion about for whom it was intended. A shell lit right between the holes of Pfc. Drozd and our Platoon Medic, Pfc. Lynch. Both men got tiny pieces of shell fragments in their noses. Other than that, no one else, to my knowledge, was hurt.

Soon a shell burst off to our left and three canisters of blue smoke went bouncing across the field in front of us. Our artillery, indeed was going to work. Several more smoke shells burst between us and the town. In a matter of seconds, the whole ares was cloaked in a heavy cloud of blue smoke. It was like looking through a heavy fog. Apparently, what was happening was that an enemy force was moving to outflank us and our artillery was throwing smoke to cover our retreat. We were pulling out!!

It was good to be on the move again. We left our positions one man at a time, keeping well bent over and running swiftly past abandoned foxholes and equipment left behind by the retreating men. The last man to leave the area was Captain Powers. As I passed, he was sitting tensely on the ground beside the radio. His Jeep driver, Pfc. Mascara and his radio man, Pfc. Bistline stood close by. I almost smiled at the worried look on Captain Powers face. The situation did not look good.

The first platoon crossed the canal and proceeded to move down the far bank. As we began to run through the smoke, a machine-gun opened up behind us. I could see the tracers speeding past. A mortar shell knocked a limb off a tree almost over my head, but I kept on, ignoring it.

Up ahead the canal made a bend to the left and again to the right, making sort of a figure "S". This is where the machine-gun was concentrating it's fire. We all had to pass this spot in order to keep in the shelter of the embankment. I learned the next day that Sgt. Byrom, from North Carolina, was shot through his temple while trying to get around this bend. He had been Sgt. for about three days and, like the rest of us had high hopes of living through the war. He was, in my humble opinion, one of the best looking men in our company. He was married, but other than that, I don't know much about him. On our way, by troop train, to our Port of Embarkation, we passed through his home town, within sight of his house. I had felt sorry for him to be saying good-bye to his home like that. It would have been better not to have seen it at all.

I saw the body of a dead soldier in the uniform of an American Tanker, lying on his back on the opposite bank of the canal. He clutched the brim of his helmet in his still hand.

Well, this retreat was more or less orderly. We finally came to a large open area, where we dispersed and I sat down to eat a "K" ration which I had been carrying in the bloused leg of my trouser.

It was getting dark when Sgt. Huff gave the order for us to assemble. We did so, reluctantly, for most of us were tired and sore from the run we had made just an hour before. We followed Huff back to the canal where we were told to dig in. I was still wet with sweat, but had become quite cold during our rest so the exercise of digging felt good.

Since the ground was frozen, it was quite a job to get through the first six inches, but once through the frozen crust, I made good progress. Digging rapidly, I left only enough room at the top of my hole to get my entrenching tool past my body. Some of the time I would lay on the ground and dig with my hands. Since it was by now dark, I had to dig by feel. I soon had enough space that I could sit down with my knees under my chin and not have my head show above ground.

By now I was exhausted. I almost fell asleep in this cramped position when I remembered that I was supposed to arrange the guard schedule. After the first guard was posted, I dropped by the foxhole of Pfc. Drozd for a visit. He had brought with him a Kraut blanket that he had somehow found in the area that we had vacated that afternoon. Together we divided the blanket with a bayonet and I took my half to my foxhole. A light snow, with large feathery flakes, was beginning to fall. They were wet and melted almost as soon as they hit. I was very glad to have my half of the blanket, even though it still had the pungent body odor of the German soldier who had owned it before me. I placed the blanket carefully over my hole, weighting one side down with loose dirt and stones so that I could crawl down and pull it securely over my head. I was pleased to find that the hole was very comfortable, though cramped. When the guard woke me to relieve him, I found that the hole had been so warm that my glasses were all fogged up.

It was about midnight when I went on guard. It was still snowing a bit, but not bad. It was black as pitch as I walked back and forth between the foxholes, ever alert for suspicious sounds or movement.

Three rapidly fired shots rang out from across the canal. This was the agreed danger signal in case the listening post sensed enemy presence. There was a sudden "Pfffttt!" I stopped dead in my tracks, trying to figure out what the sound was and where it came from. All of a sudden there was a loud "crack", and all the surrounding area was bathed in a brilliant white light. A parachute flare!!! I remembered my training while back in the States, and remained motionless until the flare burned itself out as it floated to earth. A time that seemed like an eternity. I soon regained my composure and resumed my guard post, pacing back and forth between the foxholes filled with sleeping comrades.

Another "Pfffttt!" and another "crack" and the brilliant white light again made me feel like I was naked in front of an auditorium filled with people. This time, instead of freezing, as I was taught, I moved very slowly to a prone position on the ground.

The machine-gun on the bend in the canal began to fire. Tracer bullets split the night an a "Buurrp", answered. Yes, Jerry was there and not very far from where I lay either. The awesome sound of the Burp gun, sent me looking for my hole. The last flare had burned out and my eyes had not yet become accustomed to the darkness as I groped around in an effort to find my safe haven. Since I had not allowed the dirt to pile up around the hole, when I dug it, but spread it around to avoid easy detection by the enemy, and had pulled the blanket over it when I went on guard, I now had difficulty in finding it. When I did, I sat on the ground and let my feet hang into the hole. I was sitting in this position when Sgt. Juan came down the line, waking the men as he came. He stopped and chatted with me for a minute. "We're being attacked," he told me, "Keep the men awake and on the alert." With that he retreated into the darkness from which he had come.

Sgt. Hugh Forkham, of the Second Platoon, was in charge of the heavy machine-gun crew that were making all the noise. The firing kept up for about an hour. Chandler, Kitchen and Bark had all been detained to a listening post across the canal. I hated to see Chandler get this assignment, as I knew that all three of these men had been in trouble with Sgt. Huff the week before. Now there was a good chance that none of them would get back.

All at once I heard a blood curdling scream. I don't think that I will ever forget it. "Oh, oh," I thought, "someone just got bayonetted in his foxhole." My concern for Chandler rose. It had sounded like his voice. The next day, I learned that it had been Ralph, "Kid" Bratcher, that had made the sound. He had fallen asleep sitting on the edge of his foxhole. He was having a bad dream, an when Sgt. Juan came to check on him, he thought that he was being attacked by a German. He started crawling on his hands and knees for the canal with Sgt. Juan astride his back. The funny part of it all was that Drozd heard the noise and started out after them with his rifle ready for action. They laughed about it later, but if some of the men I know had been in Drozd's situation, they would have probably shot and asked questions later.

The yellow tracer bullets were still blazing off to the north, where Sgt. Forkham had laid down his F.P.L. (Final Protective Line) The answering "Brrrrpp" of the Jerry Burp gun was still persistently present. Finally the shooting stopped and things became quiet again. We didn't know if the platoon up ahead had been wipe out, or if they had beaten off the attack. At any rate, I remained motionless in my foxhole, listening and straining every ounce of my being, trying to catch some sound, or movement which might betray the presence of our enemy.

In the grey dawn, which was beginning to break, I could make out an object on the opposite canal bank, that looked suspiciously like a German helmet. I took aim at it a couple of times, but didn't fire as it did not move, I held my fire. As the light became brighter, I made out the outline of a tree stump. I relaxed in the knowledge that at least there was no danger from this object.

I settled back into my cramped foxhole and pulled the blanket over the opening. Sleep crept up on me and the next thing I knew, I awoke with a start, wondering what was going on outside. To my surprise, I could not move my body. I could barely move my arms. I felt like a snake which had been hibernating all winter. I was thoroughly chilled through and through. From my hips down I had absolutely no feeling. The tight foxhole, my wet clothing and the cold had cut off my circulation so that the lower part of my body felt like it was paralyzed. With great effort, I was able to pull myself up with my arms. I stood leaning on the edge of my hole, blinking at the bright light of day. The sky was not that bright, but coming from my dark foxhole, as I had, it was too bright to look at without squinting. Standing felt good, and as circulation began to return to my lower body I found that I could now swing my legs back and forth a little. Pulling myself out onto the sloping canal bank, I tried to stand. My knees buckled and I almost fell to the ground. I felt weak as a baby. After standing awhile, and swinging my legs back and forth, I found that I could walk, although I staggered like a drunk. It took about a half-hour of moving about before I was able to walk normally. To this day, my left knee feels the affects of this nights sleep, whenever the weather is particularly cold and damp.

Chandler had not returned from his assignment to the listening post on the other side of the canal. I sat on the edge of my hole and opened a "K" ration. It didn't taste good. I took only a few bites and stuffed the remainder into a pocket of my field jacket. As I sat there reminiscing about the night before, Pfc. Levitt, from the second platoon, came by with a box of machine-gun ammunition in each hand and his carbine slung over his shoulder. I was overjoyed to have someone to talk with. He told me of the night before, how the German patrol had come down the canal in rubber boats, with some of them walking beside them on the bank. They had paddled and walked right into the machinegun position. A couple of them were killed in the initial burst. After the firing stopped, a wounded Kraut made so much noise, calling for a medic, that Sgt. Forkham went out and "dispensed" with him. During the fire fight, Levitt said,

Sgt. Forkham had burned out one of the water cooled machine guns. No anti-freeze had been provided, as recommended, and the gun had been fired dry. Forkham had calmly kicked the useless weapon over the bank, into the canal and went to work firing the other gun which was properly cooled. It had been quite a night for the second platoon. They had had no casualties as far as I could determine.

After a bit more conversation with Levitt, he continued on his way with his ammo. I was once more alone with my thoughts which were not very comforting. Of course the enemy knew exactly where we were now. Even though the information cost them several lives they had obtained all the information they required and now we waited to see what they would do with it. We didn't have to wait long. I heard the whistle and rush of artillery shells and dived for my foxhole. Sure, he knew exactly where we were. The shells burst in the area that our CP occupied.

Between barrages, I began to munch on a chocolate bar that I had saved from my earlier ration. The inside of my mouth was raw from eating these bars and the hard "K" ration candy. I had to do something to occupy the time, so I just kept on munching. The shells were coming in sporadically so that it wasn't safe to venture from our holes. After one particularly heavy barrage, I heard Pfc. Drodz yell. I looked over to where he was and saw him holding up his sleeping bag. It was riddled through and through with shell fragments. It had the appearance of an old feather pillow on which the moths had done a number. Drozd was laughing. It was good to see another human and hear someones voice, especially someone who could still smile and laugh. I laughed with him and it felt good. "What if you had been in it?" I asked. This brought another smile, but our conversation was cut short by more "incoming mail." At the sound of the ominous rush, we both ducked back into our protecting holes. I felt uncomfortable in my tight quarters, so I began digging to improve them. I would dig until tired, then let up until the next shell hit, inspiring me to dig down another six, or more inches. Soon I had a hole long enough to lie down in. The entrance was barely large enough for me to enter and leave with my ammunition belt and attached equipment. The frozen ground overhead made good protection from anything but a direct hit from the searching artillery of our foe. I fashioned shelves along the sides of the excavation to hold my gas mask, grenades and extra rations. It was now a comfortable home away from home.

All day the tension in the air had grown. Our artillery, which had been going over our heads and hitting the German held woods to our front, now was creeping up on our flank, with an ominous steadyness which spelled disaster. The enemy artillery shells had ceased falling in our area, but the murderous friendly barrages moving slowly from our left to right, could only mean one thing. Jerry had mounted an enveloping movement in broad day-light. Looking across the canal, I saw something that I had not noticed before. There in the wide open field stood at least six American tanks. They were painted white to blend with the snow, which by now was completely melted. The white tanks now stood out very clearly. I felt a feeling of security go through me and I breathed a bit more easily. These tanks will surely make our position a lot safer. When I looked again, some time later, they had not moved an inch and I came to the conclusion that they were all knocked out. When and how this happened, I hadn't a clue.

The friendly artillery fire was still creeping up on our southern flank, marking the progress of the encircling enemy attack. The uncertainty of it all, and the fact that I had not seen any of our senior non-coms or officers all day, gave me an overwhelming sense of loneliness. I re-read my latest letters from home, and tore up and buried the envelopes. Then I settled down to look at the pictures which I carried in my billfold. I no one but a soldier who has been away from home for a long time can realize the value of those pictures when in a situation like we found ourselves in this afternoon. It was almost like seeing all of the folks in the pictures again.

Now there was nothing to do but sit and think. Think—that is the worst thing that a soldier can do in combat. That is the reason that so many of our hospitals are flooded with soldiers who are mentally affected with Post Trauma Syndrome. They have had too much time alone in which to think. Action, and the sights of battle never hurt anyone. It's the period afterwards when a man gets a chance to let his mind dwell on those things that hurt him emotionally. My thoughts this afternoon were mostly of home, friends and family. I remembered that my brother Leslie, who had completed a tour of duty in Alaska, as a gunner/radio man on a B-26 bomber, was now Stateside and had just experienced the birth of his first son on Christmas Eve. Life still seemed to be worth living, but right now the problem was to get out of this situation alive.

The friendly artillery barrages were still creeping ominously around us, tracing the route of the encircling enemy forces. The barrages were furious. Heavy clouds of dust and smoke arose whenever the large caliber shell would burst. The tension inside me was mounting steadily. I felt like screaming. I knew what was going on and felt helpless to stop it. It would be only a matter of a few hours now, and we would have to face the enemy in a showdown. We would either fight to the end, or be captured. The later did not seem like a reasonable option.

All at once the air was filled with the roar of many engines. Looking up I saw the graceful formation of a squadron of P-47's. What a beautiful sight!! As they passed over our positions on their reconnaissance pass, they still were at a high altitude. I confess that my eyes filled with tears and I cried. I also thanked God for these beautiful deliverers. I'm not particularly proud of my emotional reactions, but I tell it that my readers may understand some of the strain and mental anguish that we had to endure. I often felt that a pitched battle would have been preferred rather than the strain of just sitting and waiting to see what the enemy would do next. As the planes passed over at their cruising altitude, the sky was filled with the bursts of anti-aircraft fire which literally blackened the sky. The small, 20mm bursts were punctuated here and there with the larger, blacker bursts of the heavy shells. The first two dive bombers peeled off from the formation and went screaming down with their guns blazing. No cowards, these "Fly-Boys." There may has well been no anti-aircraft fire for all they cared. They carried out their mission without seemingly caring about personal safety one little bit.

We could see their tracers bounce off the ground a ricochetted into the air again. I shouted, I cheered, just like a fan at a football game. "Hit the so and so's!" I shouted excitedly. "Don't let one of them get away!" This was real war, and though right now I had a grandstand seat, I knew that every shell, every bullet and every bomb involved me. They were out to get me, and they would if someone didn't get them first. My attitude toward life was changing. I wanted a chance to mix it up with them! The Germans in this area had had it their way long enough. They had killed and captured almost a third of our division and knocked out about every tank we owned. They still had the upper hand. Until our dive bombers came, that is.

The big air show had begun. The P-47, Thunderbolts, came in in pairs. We watched as they would peel off from the formation, and doing a wing-over, come diving through the anti-aircraft fire that was thick enough to walk on. Their eight guns were blazing as they dove on their target which was unseen by our eyes. They left long trails of smoke from burnt powder from their guns. When the planes were at tree-top level, we could see them release their bombs. Two at a time, one on each side of the road, so, I was told, calculated to catch a tank, or other vehicle in between. A later report said the three tanks were knocked out in this action. Many troops must have been destroyed as well. The attack was turned back!

The second platoon was filing past us now. They were going up the canal to guard a bridge where the enemy was expected to cross in case of a counter attack. This left me in the foxhole that I thought would be first in line if the enemy did come from the east. I found out later that Sgt. Forkham still had his heavy machine-gun squad in position between me and any attack from that direction.

The friendly artillery barrages were now falling between us and the town of Herrlisheim. We were cut off on three sides and our only escape route would be covered by so much enemy artillery fire that to make a break for safety would be like committing suicide. All we could do was wait.

I thought I saw some running figures about a thousand yards up the canal. As I looked, the area was enveloped in a sheet of flame, smoke and flying debris. When the smoke and dust settled there was no more sign of life. Our artillery had done a remarkable job.

All firing had ceased, and though no enemy was in view, I still had a feeling that all was not well. I didn't know what was wrong, but the sight of the disabled tanks in the field across the canal and the smell of burnt powder in the air was anything but reassuring. I sat on the edge of my foxhole for about an hour, just thinking and nibbling at a dry ration biscuit.

The day was getting late and the sky was becoming overcast. It looked like more snow was due. Occasional mortar shells would come whispering in and burst in the area near the C. P. Whenever I heard their ominous sound I would seek the friendly protection of my hole. Each time I would grit my teeth and wait, clenching my fists and waiting till the nerve racking explosions told me that the danger was past. They always said that you wouldn't hear the shell that got you, but I wasn't so sure. Most of the men that got hit didn't live to tell if they heard the shell coming or not. Just to make sure, I ducked.

I had on my wrist, an old dog tag chain. I had worn it since I left the states. I felt that this was my good luck charm. I had convinced myself that when the chain broke, my number would be up. Well, I was toying with the chain this afternoon and it broke. I'll never allow myself to become so superstitious about anything again. I was frantic when I found that the chain had come apart. I worked feverishly to repair it. Luckily, I did get it back together and wore it for about two days. As soon as we got out of the combat area, I threw the thing as far as I could.

Looking toward the town of Herrlisheim, along the canal, I saw two white objects moving towards us. Looking closely, I could make out the shapes of two tanks. They weren't ours, of that I was sure. As I watched, they came steadily on. About fifty yards from my foxhole, was an artillery F. O. crew's abandoned half-track. Beside this vehicle, was a field telephone, which, I assumed, was connected to our company command post. PFC Levitt was on his knees furiously turning the crank. Leaving my foxhole, I walked over to the vehicle to see what luck he was having. We tried several times to get through to Captain Powers, but to no avail. The tanks were now on our side of the canal and we could make out running figures of several infantry men ahead of them. The ominous force came steadily on. I looked at Levitts dirty, unshaven face. "I guess this is the way and infantry company goes out," he said in disgust, and kicked the useless telephone to one side. The way the enemy force was headed, they would cut us off completely from our officers and the situation being what it was, appeared to far gone to mend. "Take off like a ruptured duck and tell the Captain that the Jerry tanks are coming," he said. The prospect of moving a little sounded good to me. I lit out at a dead run, bent over and zig-zaging as I had been trained to do. In full view of the enemy troops, I dashed in the general direction of the C. P. I wasn't sure where it was, but I came upon Captain Powers walking along the edge of a depression in which he had set up his base of operations. No doubt he thought I was making a break for freedom for he put his hand on his pistol and demanded, "Where are you going?" Believe it or not, I saluted right out there in the field and said calmly, "Sir, two Jerry tanks are coming up the canal." "Are you sure they aren't ours?" he questioned. I laughed and he saw the foolishness of his question. "Well, take a couple of men from Headquarters and a bazooka and try to knock them out." he ordered. "Yes Sir." I replied. My heart sank. I sure asked for it this time, but I was determined to carry out my Captain's order.

I walked over to the foxhole where a bazooka team from the anit-tank platoon was huddled. They looked very serious. "The German tanks are coming and I want you two men to come with me," I said. The two men started resignedly to gather their equipment, when a bullet snapped by overhead. I was past the fear of bullets by this time, and concentrating on the task to which I had been assigned. I laughed at all the officers and men in the C. P. area as they hit the dirt. Lieutenant Hune, commander of the first platoon, finally spoke up. "Hold it, McGill. I don't think you'd better try that. Just forget about it and get back to your squad." Why he took it on himself to reverse the Captains order, I'll never know. We had all hated his guts back in the States, but I had noticed that he had a habit of rescinding orders from higher up. He also would question statements made, by his superiors, in after battle critiques. Most of his objections seemed to make life a little easier for the enlisted men under his command. I wasn't about to argue with him on the order, and took off on a dead run it direction of my foxhole. I hadn't gone ten yards before a string of machine-gun bullet cut the air in front of me. Good sense told me toe hit the dirt. I found myself in a shallow, ice filled depression in which I was able to crawl twenty-five or thirty yards, keeping out of sight of our attackers. Finally, I ran out of depression and rose to my feet and began to run again. I don't know if anyone was shooting at me during this part of my dash. If they were, I ignored it and arrived safely back at my squads location. I was pretty winded and to my dismay, my foxhole was occupied by Tech. Sgt. Burson and Lt Olney. The only thing left for me to do was to find another hole and crawl in. Soon smoke shells began to fall in the area between our foxholes and the C. P. White phosphorus shells were bursting within thirty yards of my position, but across the canal from me. By now I could plainly see some of the German Infantry and occasional bullet were spitting the air.

There was a deafening crash and a sheet of flame appeared in the branches of a tree directly over Sgt. Forkhams machine-gun position. A tree burst, directly over the old position of the second platoon. I thought that it was a lucky thing that they had vacated. To my surprise, I saw a movement along the edge of the canal, and saw Tech/Sgt. Grebl and Sgt. Tarola emerge dragging Sgt. Forham by the armpits. Forkhams lips were covered with a bloody froth and his usually red face was much redder than usual. He was a heavy man, weighing, I would judge, in the area of two hundred and fifty pounds. I could see that the two men dragging him were having quit a time. "Give us a hand," Sgt. Grebl ordered. Leaving the comparative safety of my hole, I went out and took hold. Crawling on our hands and knees, so as not to attract attention from our attackers, we dragged Sgt. Forkaham to my hole. Once in the hole, we shook his hand and apologized for not being able to help him further. We all thought that his leg was broken, and judging from the bloody froth around his mouth, he must have internal injuries. The tree burst had broken off a large tree limb which had fallen on him and pinned him to the ground. The two non-coms had fortunately been able to move the limb and to drag him clear of the position.

I had been ordered, by Lt. Olney to move my men out whenever the rest of the company began to evacuate their positions. By now the smoke, from our friendly artillery, was quite thick, and the men from my own and other platoons, were retreating in a disorderly manner. All semblance of control of the men had vanished. It was every man for himself. I, for one did not feel that I wanted to stand and fight. I was quite sick of the war, but was now resigned to my fate, which seemed sure to be death within a few minutes.

As the head men of my squad began to move out on a run, I dropped to my knees and emptied my rifle at the oncoming figures. Jamming another clip into the magazine, I emptied it again and again. I was satisfied to see the running figures, of our attackers, disappear from view. The rapidity with which I had fired, must have made them think that they had hit our main line of resistance and that we were ready to give battle. At least it held them up for a few minutes.

By this time, the two Mark Four tanks were within rifle range. I could see the upper half of the tank commanders protruding from the open turrets. It would have been easy to shoot either one of them, had I been in that frame of mind, but I reasoned that as long as they hadn't fired on us, there was no reason to attract their attention in case of a miss.

Up to this point, the enemy infantry had been ahead of the tanks. Now the drivers were gunning their motors and shifting gears. They were passing up their rapidly approaching foot soldiers. It was time for me to start moving! I had always considered myself a good runner, but here I was behind all the rest of the company. I had abandoned all of my equipment, save for my rifle, ammunition and a grenade or two. My heavy clothes and shoepacks weighed a ton. It was only a matter of a few rods of running, before the beads of perspiration began to run down my face and cloud my glasses. The two German tanks, with their exposed commanders, were within easy rifle range now. I called to my squad leader, who was carrying the bazooka. He laid it down and I took it. Holding the weapon, I made a snap decision. The tanks had not fired a round as yet, why antagonize them and draw fire by a missed rocket fired from this weapon. "No," I told myself, "I'm not going to be a dead hero." Throwing the bazooka to the ground, I again joined my comrades in what was to be a run for our lives.

During the time that the German tanks had been coming up behind us, one of our light tanks with a 75mm. assault gun, from our Headquarters company, had been moving back and forth in the background, trying to attract their attention. I'm sure that this is one of the reasons that they had not fired on us, the infantry. I didn't know the full story till later, but I know that only the hand of God could have kept one of the German tankers from pressing the trigger on his machine-gun and slaughtering us like so many animals, in true Nazi style.

The ruse of the light tank had worked. They had succeeded in drawing the enemy's attention away from the routed doughboys, who were, by now, rapidly putting distance between them and the dreaded tanks.

To my surprise, I spotted Sgt. Forkham. He was limping doggedly along. He was without helmet or weapon. His injured leg appeared very stiff, but even with this handicap, he was making good time. I was much encouraged to see him alive, after having given him up as a victim of the war. His lips were still covered with the bloody froth, but he was not about to give up. I shouted to him. "Good boy, Forkham, an old soldier never dies." Two of his men went over to him and put their arms around him and helped him into a jeep which had pulled swiftly up and then disappeared just as swiftly, bearing him and all the doughboys that could cling to it.

The valiant tank, which had been drawing the German tankers attention, once more made its dash from one clump of trees to the next. Something screamed past me and I saw the sheet of flame as it leaped skyward. The tank immediately became a flaming torch. A good shot from the tank of the Feurer. From later reports, we learned that only one man escaped. His name was Leitheizer, later decorated for his actions. I owe my life to those who died in that holocaust, as do many of the men of "B" company.

Looking back over my shoulder, I could see the white painted Jerry tanks were now "hull defalade," with only the turrets with the big guns showing above ground level. Fortunately for us, they could not bring their bow guns to bear on us, as they were now below the line of sight.

Suddenly, the sound of bullets split the air and a stream of tracers passed to my right. They were at least fifty yards away from me, so I just kept on running. The ground around me was flat as a pancake. I was desperately looking for a place to lie in case the bullets came any closer. Each burst from the enemy machine-gun was coming closer, and I knew that soon they would be aimed at me. Thank Goodness, the enemy was forced to use the co-axial guns, which means that they could not be reversed without moving the turret in which they were mounted along with the cannon. When the next ???eam of lead passed within about twenty yards, I figured it was time to hit the dirt. This I did, and ???at in time. According to Pfc Birtch, who was behind me, a stream of bullets passed directly over ???, kicking up dirt behind and in front of my position. Not one even touched me.

We learned later that Pfc Lipstreuer was seriously injured by one of the tank shells. Someone ???d they had seen his body with its puffed eyes and blood running from his nose and ears, the way ???n look when they die of concussion. One leg, obviously broken, was lying up beside him. Ken had been married about a month before we left for overseas. I had never been very initiate with him. He ???s just one of those fellows who you were always running into at chow call or mail call and on special details. Always doing his job. What a joy to learn, many years after the war, that he had not ???d, but lay for several days in a semi-conscious way, until discovered by two young German soldiers who took him captive and got him to a hospital where his leg was removed and he received ???nane treatment.

The light was growing dim now, and with the smoke screen that our artillery had provided, it seemed like twilight. The burning American tank was blazing away like a fiery beacon off to my right. Figures of running men thought the fog, made a vivid picture, which I will not soon forget.

The tanks behind us were firing furiously, now with everything they had. I was angry now to the point where I didn't care if they shot me or not. Once I dropped the warm scarf, that my family had sent me as a Christmas gift, and went back to pick it up. I knew that if I did, I might not ever need a scarf again, but I also knew how good it felt on cold nights standing guard.

I passed Lt. Colonel Clayton Wells, commander of the 66th AIB and of later Dillingen bridge fame. He was pacing back and forth by his jeep in about the only low spot in that whole area. I had to smile. The big brass didn't look so fearsome out here. He too was human and at this time he probably was as desperate as we were. I kept to the right, to avoid the main body of the company. I crossed another canal by means of a narrow foot-bridge. There was no water in it and I could have easily walked across on dry land instead of making silhouette of myself as I did. At this point, I really didn't care if one of those trigger happy Krauts was close enough to take a pot shot at me. I still had two chances. He might miss and then again I might get one of those "million dollar" wounds that would mean a quick trip back to the States. At any rate, I didn't care. This had been a complete route, not a strategic withdrawal. We had left all of our equipment, including our bedrolls and canteens. I was ???g from thirst. My clothes were soaked in sweat and when I finally slowed down to a walk, I put my precious warm scarf around my neck as insurance against catching cold.

I was approaching the outskirts of the town of Wyersherm when two unfamiliar soldiers in the uniform of the American Army stepped out in front of me. "Hold it up soldier, where do you think you're going? Give the password." Hysterically I told them that we hadn't been given the password and that the whole German Army was just a few blocks behind me. "Get some tanks, quick," I pleaded. The two soldiers just looked at each other and shrugged. I hollered and plead with them till I guess they thought I was nuts. One of them answered calmly, "Cool down soldier, don't worry, if we can see them we'll shoot them. We're from the Thirty-sixth Division and we're here to relieve you guys." With that they let me go on my way into the town.

I was glad to see some of our company vehicles parked close to the buildings that lined the narrow street. Here I met Tony Marino, from McBrides machine-gun squad as he came toward me down the street. It was good to see someone that I knew again. One by one, the boys came in, Petrin, Bratcher, Szymoniac, McBride and a couple of others. All this time I was wondering what had become of Chandler. I hadn't seen him since he went on outpost duty the night before.

Now an important thought entered my head. "Where can we find something to eat?" I couldn't remember when I had eaten last, but my stomach was sending signals that it needed to be filled. After some questioning, we were directed to a field kitchen set up on the steps of a large stone building. We didn't know what outfit the kitchen belonged to, but we borrowed mess gear from the cooks and men standing around, and got in line. I don't know, to this day, whose chow-line it was, but it didn't matter. This was the first hot food we'd smelled, or eaten for many days. We didn't question the ability of the cooks nor did we bother ourselves with ettequete. I do recall that there was a lot of lumpy potatoes and some cold meat with plenty of apple sauce and G. I. coffee. Delicious!! Probably one of the most memorable meals of my entire military career.

After doing justice to the food, the next thing we wanted was sleep. By now it was pitch dark, but we ran into several men from the Third Platoon who said they knew where the biggest part of the company was located. They lead us to the stairway to a large winceller. The cellar was very secure, in that the ceiling consisted of one great stone arch. Not unlike a bomb shelter. Flashlights and matches were flickering and cigarettes glowed in the dark. We could hear the muffled voices of the men below, as they reveled in their new security and rested after the long run from our battlefield positions. It was a different world than what we had known the past few days. We located more of the Third Platoon men and soon we made for the wine casks. The long gruelling run had given us a consuming thirst, and no water was at hand. After all had slacked their thirst, we relaxed on top of a pile of potatoes. Now becoming quite chilled from our damp cloths, Marino and I curled up together under and old feather filled quilt.

From time to time, we would hear new arrivals enter the celler and the air remained heavy with tobacco smoke.

It didn't take long to get to sleep. One hour ago we had been running for our lives, without expecting to live the next minute out, now we were warm and full of food. Some of the men were even laughing about their experiences of the last few days. I was too exhausted to care for anything. I envisioned a troop of German soldiers coming stomping down those stairs at any moment. That was of little concern right now. All I wanted was sleep—sweet sleep. I was dead tired.

Someone awakened us at about one o'clock. We were warm from the mutual heat of our bodies. It just didn't seem that anything could be important enough to waken us at this unearthly hour. Grudgingly, we threw off the quilt and groped for our weapons. As far as I knew, Chandler had not shown up yet. From somewhere near the base of the stairway, someone was saying, "We're moving out, men, pick up all your equipment and come upstairs for briefing." Upstairs, the men stood around a large room with a stove blazing merrily in one corner. Already, men were lighting up, and the room was becoming heavy with smoke. Soldiers were leaning on their rifles and some of them looked like they were about to fall asleep in that position. Some of them slid to the floor along the wall. The room was crowded, but I found a space in the inconspicuous corner behind the cozy stove.

A tank officer came in and after checking the black out curtains, turned to the motley, unshaven, bone weary men. "We have just been officially relieved by the Thirty-sixth Division," he began, "we will move out and proceed to our old billets near Hochfelden, there the Division will be reorganized." Occasional bursts of incoming artillery would shake the building, and men would visibly tighten in their places, but no-one spoke.

I fell gloriously asleep in my quiet, inconspicuous corner, and woke to find the men filing out into the cold darkness. All the lights in the room were out, save for the cheery glow of the stove. I was perspiring from the heat of the stove and the cold air felt good on my brow. Somehow, I found my way to our squad vehicle. There, waiting for me, was the rest of the squad. "What happened to you?" someone asked. I didn't tell them that I had had enough war for one time and had gone back to town on my own, as I assumed the rest of the company was doing. I found out later that Captain Powers had held the line with twenty men in a ditch about five hundred yards out of town. The Germans had come so close that they had shouted taunts at our men. One of them had shouted in fair English. "You guys ran tonight, you'll run again in the morning." From what we heard later they hit a brick wall the next day when they ran head on into the Thirty-sixth Division in dug in positions

The Twelfth Armored Division had done it's job at a tremendous cost of men and machines. It had also won its new name, "The Suicide Division," and a lot of respect from the German Army.

We were all conscious of the hopeless feeling that comes from being defeated. We had been beaten and beaten bad. I don't think it entered anyones mind that we were lucky to be alive right then. The pain of losing was too great.

The ride back to our old billet was anything but pleasant, but just the idea that we were pulling off the line was some consolation. It was cold in the half-track and snow was falling. We could hear the shells bursting behind us, and were much relieved when we felt that we were out of range. Nerves were on edge and the men were in a bad mood. Everyone snarled and shouted at his fellow squadmembers. A lot of things were said that were not meant. When you've been facing death constantly for four days without sleep or hot food, one doesn't think much of hurting a friends feelings.

I thought the ride would never end, but finally the vehicle halted. It was just at the crack of dawn and we could see that we were back in the little town from whence we had left a few day earlier. What a different bunch of men!! We had learned that the war against the Nazi didn't always go according to the way we would have liked it.

The end of the war seemed a long way off, and right now, the winner seemed to be anyones guess.

During the first week of February, 1945, we moved south. Under the command of General DeTassigny, of the Free French Army, and with the American Third and Twenty-eighth Infantry Divisions, we made contact with a French, Moroccan Division, moving up from the south and effectively wiped out the Colmar Pocket, that had been a challenge to the French for several months.

Chapter IV

COLMAR POCKET

"OK, MOUNT UP". The voice of Lt. Huff was heard above the muffled hum of many motors. "We'll be traveling under black-out conditions, so be sure that each car commander keeps a sharp lookout for the vehicle ahead. We don't want any rear-enders and if you get too far back, you might lose the column."

The half-tracks were lined up on the street across from the house where we had billited just a week earlier. The little town of Niederhausbergen is about five kilometers northwest of the city of Strasbourg in Alsace and within view of the twin spires of the Strasbourg Cathedral.

Rifle butts clanged noisily and webbing creaked as the "Doughs" entered the dark interior of the vehicle and found their seats along the sides, facing each other. It was February and the weather had been miserable enough that we were glad to have been housed in relatively comfortable quarters since the ordeal at Herrlisheim. The route at Herrlisheim had unnerved and dampened the spirits of many of the men in the third platoon. But here we were about to launch on another campaign to end the seemingly endless war.

The information given earlier that afternoon was that, as part of General Middleton's Sixth Corps, the Twelfth Armored was now to become part of the French First Army commanded by General DeTassigny. The American Third and Twenty Eighth Infantry Divisions were to break through the Colmar Pocket. The armor was to attack and exploit the area exposed by their success. Chances of bottling up the German troops in the Vosges Mountains were good. The French First Division was to move up from the south and link up with us someplace south of Colmar.

In the unheated half-track, the only warm place to sit is on the floor plates between the driver and car commander. The rest of the squad gets warmth from each other and from the cigarettes that most of them smoke. All in all, the back compartment of the vehicle is drafty and cold under any conditions. Mutterings and griping by the incarcerated individuals is not unusual and even an occasional cuss word is heard.

This was the scene as the darkness gathered and the arm signal to depart was passed from vehicle to vehicle. Slowly, like a giant serpent, the column began to move. As the vehicles gathered speed the house and the little Alsatian village faded from view.

I sat on the warm plates between our driver, T-5 Sigismund Ryfinski and the squad leader S/Sgt. Don Juan. Juan was standing in the car commander's position with the .50 caliber machine-gun at his side. My mind went back to the past weeks since Herrlisheim. B-Company had not sustained the casualties that the sister companies had in that great fiasco, due to our good fortune to be chosen to be in reserve. However there had been casualties and the past weeks had been spent in indoctrinating replacements and obtaining new equipment. I had personally lost my bedroll, overcoat, web equipment and bayonet in the mad dash across the open field under fire of the two German tanks. We made it and were still alive and that was all that counted.

In the past weeks there had been several reconnaissance patrols and a screening operation for the Fourteenth Armored Division. They had received a major shellacking at a town called Hatton. They needed our help to maintain forward elements to blunt the initial thrust of any enemy attempt to break through.

A week ago, we had moved into the little town of Niederhausbergen. Someone had remarked "in this part of the world, the smaller the town, the larger the name". We had parked our half-track in the driveway of a comfortable looking bungalow and while Sgt. Juan attended a meeting for squad leaders, I was given the assignment of finding billets for the squad.

As I tried the door to the house, a crowd of children gathered to watch. My knocks were getting no answer and as I turned away, a plump, red-faced middle aged housefrau approached. Somehow she smugly informed me that the frau of the house was not home. At that point, I asked "haben se der schussel?" to which she replied "nicht". I turned and prepared to give the door my very effective boot treatment. At this point the rosy cheeked woman fairly shouted "nicht, ich haben der schussel!" When I seemed to respond, she hurried away to the house next door and promptly returned with the key. The door opened revealing a hospitable, well kept kitchen. A parade of doughs passed through, laden with bedrolls, mussette bags, rifles and the usual articles of comfort. The Second Squad, led by S/Sgt. Bob Edwards had arrived and notified us that they had been ordered to share our "spacious" quarters. His people agreed to take up housekeeping in the living room and the First Squad would reside in the kitchen/dining room area. Two items discovered in the basement were of particular interest to us. One was a keg of wine and the other a crock of delicious dill pickles.

As the troops were bedding down and sampling the goodies in the cupboards and cellar, we realized that the neighbor lady's ten year old daughter had been left to "watch the goods". Realizing why she was there, a couple of the boys began making lewd remarks and moves toward her. Even though she spoke very little, if any, english, she understood that this might not be the safest place for her. She soon took her leave, going back to the house next door.

Next day, as we were preparing a gun emplacement for the machine gun squad, I spotted a lady bicycle rider coming down the street. When she spotted the half-track in the driveway of her home, she jumped off the bike, dropping it in the middle of the street, grabbed her head with both hands and screamed "ach, mine himmel". With that she went running into her house from whence a torrent of hysterical screams were heard. Realizing that the guys in the house were not handling the situation very well, I hurried across the street and into the house. With stern hand and a threatening gesture with my rifle, the woman, still fuming, came stumbling out into the street and disappeared from view.

Things quieted down for awhile and I was about to return to the machine gun detail when a knock was heard at the door. Upon opening it, I came face to face with the woman of the house and two mature male civilians wearing arm bands with the Cross of Lorraine (official insignia of the French Free something or other) on them. These men were of military age and should have been in someone's army (either Hitler's or Gen DeGaulle's). At any rate, one of them spoke pretty good english and told us that the lady of the house had asked them to ask us to be careful of her good china and of the food supplies in the house. They said that she had found the spigot on the wine cask in her basement dripping. Someone had failed to close it completely. At this point, I was becoming irritated and walked across the room to a closet behind the kitchen stove and returned with the black SS Officers overcoat that we had found during our original "cleaning out" of the house. Holding the overcoat up for all to see, I said in my best German "her mann ist "SS" der 1st Nazi". This sobered all present and after an unintelligible conference, they turned and departed. The home proved to be one of the more comfortable billets that we enjoyed on our campaign in Europe.

The column moved steadily through the night. I realized that something was wrong. My stomach was telling me that the supper it had received before departure was not in the least acceptable. As it gurgled and boiled, I soon knew that something had to be done. Those of you who were in the army know how versatile the steel G.I. helmet is. It got a good workout that night. At least I didn't ask our driver to drop out of the convoy. When things were back to normal, I took my turn in the turret, giving directions to our driver and passing arm signals back to the track behind us. It wasn't long before Sgt. Juan decided that he too had a crisis. "Stop the vehicle" he ordered and before the half-track had fully stopped, he was on the ground running for the ditch. Well, Don Juan's session lasted for quite a while. The last red "cat-eye" of the final vehicle had long disappeared in the darkness when he returned to the half-track and we resumed our trip. "How do I know what road to take?" Ry asked as we approached a fork in the road. No one had ever told us which highway to follow and there was no way of knowing just where the enemy forces were. "I guess we better stop in the next town and wait for daylight. Better than stumbling into some kraut held town" replied Sgt. Juan.

The half-track turned off the main road and headed into a village just to our left. As we approached the shadowy buildings, there was no way of knowing who held the town. It was with a sigh of relief that we spotted two six wheeled American reconnaissance vehicles parked close to a building. No guard had been posted and when Sgt. Juan and I pounded on the door, two sleepy eyed G.I.'s responded by opening it. They had a cheery fire going in a large space heater and the 6-volt trouble light made the room look very inviting. We explained our plight and asked if we could spend the night with them and if they, in the morning, could locate our company by use of the radio. To these requests, we received positive replies. Our hosts offered us the use of an adjoining room in return for having us post a guard. I don't recall pulling guard that night but possibly because it was well after midnight when we turned in, my turn never came.

Next morning we were shown on a map where "B" Company had bivouacked for the night. Later in the morning we found them in a woods near the town of Sealstadt. Sealstadt is about twenty miles from the target city of Colmar.

"Better get your mess kits and have your guys go down to the kitchen truck, I think there still may be some grub left". It was Lt. Huff speaking. He had been somewhat perturbed with us for not keeping up during the road march. But, by noon he had cooled down and was his own "motherly" self.

After breakfast of dehydrated eggs and bacon, we returned to the half-track and tried to find something to interest us that would make the time go faster. In the distance, the sound of artillery rumbled but we were in no hurry to join the battle. Wandering through the woods, we came on a house that obviously had been used as a command post by both the German and American Forces and in that order. Signs of battle were everywhere. We came on several steel helmets with the blue-white insignia of the famous 3rd Infantry Division. They had had quite a few casualties, but the battle had not been one-sided, for lying in the woods, we found the bodies of two of Hitler's finest. One, a handsome young man with wavey black hair and the uniform of the hated SS. His right trouser leg had been cut away revealing a shrapnel wound in the thigh that nearly severed the leg. A hasty bandage had been applied, but apparently abandoned; either due to the expiration of the patient or the proximity of the 3rd Division doughboys. The second body was that of an older man, probably in his thirties. The impressive thing about him was his impeccably shined boots. I had always wanted a pair like that and laid hold of one in an effort to remove it. With much difficulty, I was able to get both boots free of the owner. It was with some chagrin that I noticed that the man's feet were wrapped in handkerchiefs for warmth. Hitler's spit and polish soldiers were not equipped for the bitter weather that they had to face hour after hour on the front. As an afterthought, the American doughboy was probably the most despicable looking creature in any man's army, but most of the time we were comfortably clothed from the soles of our sloppy but comfortable shoe packs to the hoods that buttoned to the collars of our field jackets and kept cold drafts from whistling down our necks.

At any rate, while I was struggling to get my souvenir boots, I looked up to see First Sgt. Berry and Capt. Powers watching me from their jeep as it moved slowly through the woods. I was promoted to Sgt. the next day. I don't honestly think that my lack of respect for dead Germans had anything to do with it, but then again, it might have.

When I brought my shiny boots to the half-track, Sigismund, our driver, was very emphatic. "Not in my half-track, McGill. I heard of one driver that was captured with a lot of German stuff and he was shot!". I don't recall how I got rid of the boots but I know they didn't go anywhere in Ryfinskie's half-track.

How many days we spent in the woods, I don't recall, but early Sunday morning we were ordered to issue each man "K" rations for two days and to be ready to move out by half-track within the hour. "The Twenty Eighth Division went into Colmar at first light and surprised the Germans. When one of the anti-aircraft gun crews came out to relieve the night shift, they found their position filled by American soldiers. "Sgt. Juan informed us. He had just returned from a squad leaders meeting.

We mounted up, and after the appropriate time of waiting, moved onto the highway where we joined with a company of tanks and moved steadily toward the town of Colmar.

??? past a dead German soldier lying on his back in the ditch where he had fallen, and on into town. It was snowing now and three or four inches of the light fluggy stuff was making the highway rather slippery as it melted. We passed another German body now lying in the gutter with the run-off from the snow rinsing away the blood.

It was about noon when the column came to a halt at the southern end of town. "We are ordered to attack and exploit the countryside south of Colmar" said Lt. Huff. "We expect some resistance but intelligence tells us that the main portion of the German army has taken to the Vosges mountains. We're supposed to link up with a Moroccan outfit, part of the French army, coming up from the south".

About 3:00 p.m. we were once more ordered to move out. Up till now, not a shot had been fired at us and we were feeling very fortunate.

In the distance, we could see another unit approaching a railroad track and making a dismounted attack, apparently without resistance.

We had ridden ten or twelve miles when the column stopped. "Dismount your men and fall into approach march formation. There's some kind of trouble up ahead" T/Sgt. Marion, now our platoon Sgt., informed us. "Keep spread out and follow the machine gun squad.

As we moved into the field, alongside the road a single mortar shell exploded harmlessly about a hundred yards ahead. It had been almost a month since we had been under fire and my first thoughts were "Dear Lord, how did I ever let them let me up here again". The front of the column was moving again and as we moved forward, the old trembling feeling was on me. I never knew if I was shaking from the cold, or from fear.

The column of tanks, jeeps and half-tracks was still on the road, when a group of about twelve German soldiers rounded a bend up ahead. They were double-timing with their hands on their heads and a lone G. I. with rifle ready escorting them.

A familiar figure stepped out in front of the approaching prisoners and with an arm raised ordered them to halt. I recognized the person of Lt. Col. Clayton Wells, the 66th Battalion Commander, whom I hadn't seen since I passed him in my ignoble retreat from Herrlisheim. "Put the machine gun on them!" he shouted to Sgt. Szymoniak, who was conveniently about thirty to forty yards from the road. Col. Weeks with the help of the lonely G. I. was busy lining up the Krauts facing the field where Sgt. Szymoniack was assembling his machine gun. I was sure that the next order from Col. Wells would be "FIRE!". Knowing Col. Wells as I do now, I am ashamed to admit that I thought he might commit such an atrocity. At any rate, I seriously considered charging the gun and kicking it off target, if such an order were given.

By now, several other soldiers had joined Col. Wells and were busily frisking the Germans for hidden weapons. When done, the prisoners were ordered on their way and Sgt. Szymoniak disassembled his gun and resumed the approach.

As we rounded the bend, a small village appeared immediately in front of us. On the road stood a six wheeled reconnaissance vehicle with it's tires smoldering. In the ditch, beside his foxhole, lay the body of a green-clad German soldier. An unspent Panzer-faust (bazooka) was at his side where it had fallen as it's holder died.

Two tanks pulled around the smoking vehicle and passing up the infantry proceeded toward the village. As they came to the edge of town, each turned off the road to his right. As they crossed the shallow ditch, two deafening explosions were heard. Both tanks had taken direct hits in their engine compartments. It was not immediately evident where the rounds had come from, but someone knew because it was only a few minutes before an assault gun, a light tank with a 105 mm Howitzer in the turret, rounded the bend and with a screech and squeal, came to a halt that caused the whole vehicle to rock as the driver set his brakes. In a matter of seconds, the gun was thundering as it fired round after round into what appeared to be a clump of bushes about a mile away on a hillside across a shallow valley. There was no more hostile fire as the rest of the troops and tanks moved into town.

It was almost dark now and Lt. Huff came down the line checking on the men. "We're going to hold up here for the night" he said. "Sgt. Juan, you take the first squad and set up an outpost in that white house over there". He indicated a large two story building set apart from the rest of the village, by two or three hundred feet. "McGill, you take half the squad" Sgt. Juan ordered as we approached the house. "Go around the south side and I'll take the other half to the north".

Stealthily we approached in the darkness. As my half-squad came around the house we paused, waiting for Juan and his men. Suddenly, there was the sound of running as man after man emerged from the darkness in great haste. As the last man cleared, there was a deafening blast. Sparks and fire filled the night. All was quiet except for some excited breathing. "What happened?" I asked. "We heard voices – German voices and I tried to throw a grenade through the window. It had a screen on it" replied Sgt. Juan, luckily no one was hurt.

As we ordered everyone out of the cellar, we found that they were all older men and women, except for one young man who probably was a German soldier. Because he was in civilian clothes, we ordered him along with the rest back into the "keller" and put a guard on the door to keep them there.

The rest of the night was spent on guard duty, listening for sounds of enemy movement in the darkness that enveloped the countryside. Off in the distance, I heard a duck quack and from another quadrant came an answering quack. "Oh, oh" I thought, "the enemy is approaching and using duck quacks to coordinate their attack". I almost convinced myself that this was true but as the sky began to redden in the east with approaching dawn, I decided that the sounds I had been hearing were merely coming from the barnyards of the local farmers.

A runner approached our outpost and after the approved password and countersign told us that Lt. Huff wanted us up in town where our half-track would meet us. By this time it was quite light. As we entered the town, we found that all windows were tightly shuttered and not a native was to be seen. After a short wait, our vehicle once more joined the column, moving out of town and onto the highway.

Signs of battle was everywhere evident, with burnt and damaged enemy vehicles and weapons lying in ditches. A dead horse lay in the center of the road where an Air Force strafing run had left him. The horse's rump seemed to be missing. "Must have been a direct hit", I mused, but was puzzled that the hide showed no damage. "Someone took the steaks off that one", Sgt. Juan offered, "then pulled the hide back over the bare bones".

About two in the afternoon, we entered the outskirts of the town of Rouffach. Our vehicle stopped at the formidable timber roadblock, which had been breached by lead elements of our task force. A crowd of civilians were standing around. The men were arguing about who was going to keep the logs. These logs were anywhere from eight to eighteen inches in diameter and probably fifteen feet in length; excellent material for any sawmill. As we were held up, I noticed that some of the girls were kissing the G.I.'s in the vehicle ahead. Being the adventuresome type, I grabbed the female closest to me and gave her a resounding kiss. She smiled a smile of delight, exposing a mouth with several of the front teeth missing. The last I saw her, she was still smiling and waving as our vehicle moved away. I think I made her day.

About six or eight blocks into town, our vehicle moved into a side street. The slopes of a formidable mountain came right to the edge of town. Several running German soldiers were seen scrambling through the vineyards and on up the slope. There must have been a hundred. Every weapon in our vehicle and in those adjacent were now turned on the fleeing figures. The targets soon disappeared as each individual found cover from the withering fire. "OK Marion" ordered Lt. Huff, "get a patrol together and go on up that hill. Bring back any stragglers you find".

About that time, a column of half a dozen green-clad German soldiers, with hands clasped on their heads came filing past our vehicle. Some of the enemy had decided it was safer to give up than to become a target in the shooting gallery that the hillside had become. Pfc. Russell spotted a death's head SS ring on the upraised hand of one prisoner. "Come here" he ordered. Russell pointed to the ring. The prisoner obliged by removing the ring and handing it to him.

After a considerable wait, Lt. Huff approached. "Dismount your men and find billets for them" he ordered, "this is as far as we're going to go. The Morrocan outfit has contacted our task force in the center of town, so we'll be here for awhile".

We found lodging on second floor of a large building. I don't recall what was in the downstairs, but I believe it was a business place of some sort. The first night passed without incident for our platoon. Pfc. Peeler, who had been with the patrol that climbed the hi side reported how, as they moved up the slope, he had spotted a German soldier under a tree, aiming his rifle at one of the patrol members. Instead of shooting the German, he had shouted to him. To his surprise the German dropped his rifle and put his hands up. The patrol then came on a rock quarry where a dozen or so Germans had built a fire and were busily preparing their evening meal. They either had posted no guard, or it was their guard that had given up. At any rate, our patrol had the drop on them and they surrendered without any trouble.

The next day, Lt. Huff informed us that the First Platoon had been in quite a fire fight the night before and that in the dark, Pfc. Jura had shot two Germans with one shot. Apparently a German soldier had been wounded and his buddy was trying to patch him up. As Jura spotted them in the dark, across the stone wall from him, he shot point blank not realizing that there were two.

"Get your men out to the edge of town and help the machine-gun squad set up their guns. If anymore patrols come through, we'll be ready for them" Lt. Huff ordered. "I want a twenty-four hour guard posted on both guns. You squad-leaders work out the roster".

The outskirts of town consisted of a stone wall between two terraced vineyards. The wall was about five feet high on the lower level and two feet from the higher side. It gave great protection to anyone on the lower side as only his eyes were high enough to see over, while the rest of his body was behind eighteen inches of stone and mortar.

"We can't set our gun on top of the wall", Sgt. McBride reasoned, "no one can reach it there. We'll have to notch out the wall so it will be level with the ground on the high side". We had all visually checked out the two dead German soldiers who who lay sprawled in the vineyard about four feet from the wall. Both still had on their steel helmets and both had been searched for souvenirs or important papers that intelligence might find helpful. "Prepare a spot right over the dead Krauts. That looks like the best place. Szymoniak will have his gun under that big tree about fifty yards to your left", ordered McBride.

After considerable hacking, prying and chipping, we had a notch in the wall big enough to accommodate the gun. All of this effort was done in broad daylight and in view of any curious German commanders whose troops were known to be holed up in the vicinity. In addition to this, the ammunition belt that was installed in the gun was white, to blend with a snow covered landscape. The snow on the south-facing slope had now disappeared. At night, the white belt was obvious even in complete darkness.

The first night passed uneventfully, with Chandler and me pulling a late shift from ten to twelve. The night was dark and drizzly and the rain played a mournful tattoo on the helmets of the two dead Germans in front of the gun. We were glad to return to our warm, dry billets where our sleeping bags awaited in what, to us, was sheer luxury. Even though we slept on the floor or on the ground, the sleeping bag now-a-days represented the utmost in comfort and safety.

Next day we watched as a compy of Morrocan soldiers marched by in the street below. As the formation passed, I tossed a package of cigarettes out our window as a good will gesture. A soldier broke ranks and proceeded to retrieve the pack which had landed beside their route of march. His lieutenant grabbed him by an ear and soundly booted him in his after-regions, forcing him back into line. This sort of discipline was surprising to us onlookers. American non-coms and officers were expected to treat their men with dignity. Physical contact is a "no-no". The observed manhandling of an enlisted man made us glad, once more, to be American soldiers.

About three nights later, as Chandler and I were returning to our billets, we heard the stuccato of the machine-gun which we had just left. We had been relieved at midnight by Pfc's. Querino Dentino and Anthony Marino of the machine-gun squad. "Oh, that's just those Dago's trying out the gun", Chandler rationalized. Unconcerned, we retreated to our comfortable quarters.

Two hours later, Dentino and Marino entered the room in breathless excitement. "We just took about a dozen prisoners" Dentino exclaimed. "They just about ran over us in the dark, but one of them kicked the helmet of one of their dead buddies and we started to fire. The wall got in the way so we couldn't hit anything.

They were on both sides of the wall and we couldn't traverse the gun". When we started firing, the Germans all shouted "komerad" and stopped in their tracks. Their sergeant lined them all up in the dark and had them count off. There were eighteen to start with, but only twelve made it to the stockade. The rest just slipped away in the dark. The tankers from that tank at the corner of the vineyard came over to help. Lt. Hall spotted an empty holster on one of the prisoners and asked him what he had done with his pistol. The Kraut indicated that he had left it on top of the wall when they decided to give up. Hall directed the prisoner to show him where. Someone saw the light from the lieutenant's flashlight and shouted asking who was showing the light. The answer was "Lieutenant Hall, what do you want to do about it?" To this day I marvel at our lack of concern. When we heard the machine-gun firing, the whole company should have been alerted and sent to help.

"C'mon McGill, get your squad and come with me, we're going on a little patrol" Lt. Huff ordered. "I'll be ready in a half hour. Get your men lined up. We'll go by half-track to one of the villages near by and then walk the distance to Paeffenheim. The half-track will meet us there".

"Awright you guys", I asserted, as I entered the room, "get your stuff on and be ready to leave at 1300 hours. Huff's going to take us on a little walk in the woods".

The ride to the jumping off point was uneventful and we bade farewell to our half-track driver, expecting to rondevous with him later in the afternoon.

"There's Germans back in those hills", Lt. Huff said, "our job is to look for any enemy activity in the area between this town and Paffenheim".

As we walked along the street leading out of the nameless town, we realized that our route led in a slightly uphill incline. We were rather breathless and tired of the climb when we came upon a second village, perched on the hillside. As we passed along a street, we came upon a German soldier's uniform on the sidewalk where it's owner had hastily shed it in exchange, no doubt, for a set of civilian clothes furnished by a local citizen.

Lt. Huff knocked at the door of an imposing looking residence and while I and the rest of the patrol stood with rifles ready, the door opened and an elderly gentleman stood in the doorway. With broken German, the lieutenant asked if he had seen any German soldiers, to which the man answered negatively. We were bothered by the appearance of a mature man and woman behind the man and insisted that we be allowed to interview them. Upon questioning, we were assured that these were two innocent vacationers who had come to the area to ski. Ski? no snow here, wonder where they skied. Rather than hassle with a couple of prisoners, we bade them farewell and moved on up the slope.

"I wonder what that large white building halfway up the mountain is" Lt. Huff mused. "I dunno, sir" I replied, "looks like some kind of monastery or somethin'". "We better go check it out" continued Huff, "maybe the Krauts use it for an observation post".

The climb to the objective was torturous. Rather than following roads, we took a direct route up the mountainside, through the woods, in order to avoid detection. As we approached the building the sound of a motor was heard, as of a rapidly departing vehicle. We assumed that it was one of our own, but will never know. It may have been the "other guys" leaving to avoid a confrontation.

The building did indeed turn out to be a monastery with a chapel, having one of the most ornate altar areas I have ever seen. No one in the area would admit to having seen any enemy activity and after helping ourselves to some souvenir postcards depicting the beautiful chapel, we departed single file, down a steeply sloped road, past the twelve stations of the cross. Since we were descending instead of climbing the slope, the order of the very beautiful and ornate stations was reversed, with the crucifixion first and the nativity scene last.

The road apparently would not take us into our intended objective town of Paffenheim. Leaving it, we plunged once more into the woods. As we slipped and slid down the treacherous mountain, we came upon a crude dwelling which was part cave, part shanty. It apparently had been hastily abandoned. The only food evident was a sack of potatoes. Evidence of the occupant's mode of transportation was obvious as hay and the usual stable leavings indicated that horses had been tethered nearby. Apparently, a family had used this as their hideaway, hoping that the tide of war would by-pass them.

Continuing down the hill, we were approaching a vineyard when a deafening fire fight erupted in the town. Tracer bullets were coming out of the town in all directions. Bedlam had engulfed the town.

Walking through the vineyard, we observed American troops advancing toward us in tactical fashion. A line of skirmishers was soon built up between us and the town. No one was shooting at us yet, but in response to the potentially hostile movements, Lt. Huff pulled out a white handkerchief. (All white clothing had been long since confiscated by the Army in order to prevent unintended observation by the enemy.) Apparently, Lt. Huff had ignored this regulation and had retained this handkerchief for just such an occasion as this. "Kamerad-Kamerad" Lt. Huff shouted, waving the white flag. "Kamerad-Americans, don't shoot". No one did. As we walked past the prone doughboys, we asked one of them what happened. "Don't really know, but somebody got shot and our lieutenant ordered us to secure the town. Guess they're expecting a counterattack". "Not from that direction" Lt. Huff assured them, "we've been all over the mountainside and didn't see a single Kraut".

As we moved warily into town, we spotted our "B" Company half-track. "What happened?" I asked the driver. "Some G.I. was sitting on the hood of a half-track opening a "K" ration, when a sniper shot him through the head. All heck broke loose. They shot up the town. Some guy took a flame thrower into the church and set the steeple on fire". Indeed the fire was really getting going. Black smoke and pieces of roofing now filled the air. As we watched, orange flame broke out and engulfed the wood shingle steeple with an iron cross at it's peak. In minutes the cross began to bend and then to separate from it's anchor and come tumbling to the ground. All around smiled in approval, for no doubt the sniper had been in the steeple. In the mind of the average soldier, that was always the first place to look for a sniper.

When we returned to our billets, we learned that "C" Company had been chosen to represent the infantry units of the Twelfth Armored Division in a victory parade to be held in Colmar. The festivities would be to honor General DeGaulle. We felt somewhat left out, but considering the heavy losses experienced by "C" Company during the Herrlisheim engagement, we knew that the chosen company would be a worthy representative.

The battle for the "Colmar Pocket" was over. Southern France was now secure from any major threat of Nazi military action. The prized city of Strassborg was still in American hands. Much of this success was attributable to the determination of the Hellcats of the Twelfth Armored. We had proved to the world that we were, indeed, a force to be reckoned with so far as the Nazi's were concerned. Once more the morale of our fighting men was soaring. Even though we had left many buddies behind, we were satisfied that we would contribute a great deal toward winning the war.

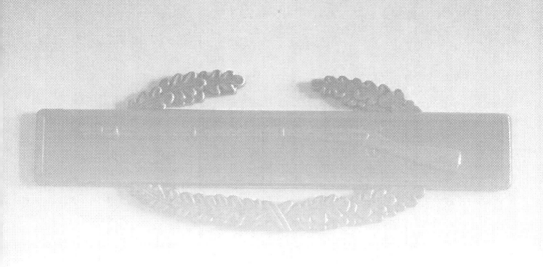

Chapter V

STERLING-WENDEL

The winter snow had disappeared from the Alsacian landscape, but the bitter wind was driving icey raindrops in our faces as we dismounted from our semi-comfortable half-tracks and followed our squad-leader across the sloping hillside to the line of tanks forming a semi-circle in the valley ahead.

"McGill, take your half of the squad and team up with the third tank in line", ordered S/Sgt. Juan in his usual brusque manner. "We'll be having a guard roster, but get your men dug in before it gets too dark".

It had been a dark day, and now as the night approached, it was hard to know just where day turned to night. The persistent rain and the flashes of artillery just over the ridge ahead gave an ominous mood to the whole situation.

As we approached our assigned tank, we were greeted by it's commander. "If you Doughs prefer, you can dig a four-man foxhole and we'll drive our tank over it for cover. You'll be a lot warmer that way". The speaker was a young man about my age and no older than most of us. We learned later that he had just made Tank Commander a few days earlier and though his tank was an older model Sherman, one that mounted a 75mm gun, rather than the newer 76mm, he was tremendously proud of his new responsibility and of his crew.

Entrenching tools came out. Chandler, Kitchen, Ell and I began in earnest to delve into the soggy, water-soaked sod. "Hey, why don't one of you use our D-handle shovel?" It was our friendly tank commander "that'd be a lot faster than those teaspoons you're using". "Good idea, thanks", I responded and proceeded to loosen the strap that held the shovel securely in it's berth alongside an axe which made up what the Army liked to call the "pioneer tools".

Dirt flew rapidly and as darkness closed in, we had a respectable excavation over which the tankers positioned their tank. Shelter halves came out and were placed around three sides of the tank to prevent cold gusts of moisture laden air from penetrating our cozy retreat. Rolling our bedrolls on the damp earth didn't present the most welcome prospect for a comfortable night's rest. "Why not use our camouflage net for a mattress?" the tank commander offered. "At least it will keep your sleeping bags dry".

About that time, a series of tremendous blasts shook the bivouac area. Flashes of fire and sparks lit up the now darkened sky. The fire seemed to come from the bowels of the earth itself. As the blasts continued, we cautiously approached the area from whence the interruption had come. After about one hundred yards had been traversed, we came to the edge of what had to be a rock quarry. In the dim light, we made out the outlines of a battery of mortars, attended by several crewmen busily dropping round after round into the tubes of the gigantic weapons. It seemed that this battery had been here for some time as shelters had been built of the cardboard shipping tubes that the ammunition had been shipped in. As the firing ceased, we moved down a steeply sloped path into the bottom of the quarry. "What kind of mortar is that?" I asked of the Staff Sergeant who seemed to be in charge. "Oh, these are 4.2 chemical mortars developed in World War I, for dispersing mustard gas. We're firing H.E. in support of the 70ᵗʰ Division's attack on Sterling-Wendel. Our curiousity satisfied, we climbed back up the path and retired to the relative comfort of our tank covered foxhole.

"McGill, you'll go on guard at ten and again at four in the morning. You'll be with Chandler. Rinquette will wake you when it's time to go". Sgt. Juan didn't stay around to shoot the breeze, but immediately faded away into the blackness of the night.

Ten o'clock came quickly and as Chandler and I took up our position about fifty yards in front of the tanks, a barrage of enemy mortar fire fell about a hundred yards in front and to our right, sending pieces of shrapnel whining through the air, in our direction. We cringed as the pieces splattered to earth and buried themselves in the wet real estate. A shiver ran down my spine and I prayed a little prayer for protection, as no one knew when or where the next fusilage would fall.

"Boy, McGill", Chandler quipped "this isn't a very good place for a guard post. They'll be trying to hit that quarry with the mortars all night. We just might get the benefit of their bad aim".

As we woke our relief team and crawled into our cozy quarters. The rain had stopped. The wind continued to blow, flapping the canvas shelter halves against the tracks and bogie wheels of the tank about. Bone weary and chilled, it wasn't long before the warm sleeping bags and soft camouflage net coaxed sweet oblivion. Sleep overcame us.

"McGill, Chandler", it was five minutes to four and Leo Rinquette from the previous shift was on his hands and knees trying to peer into the darkness beneath the tank, to awaken his relief. "Ya, Okay" I managed. The next thing I knew, it was daylight and Lt. Huff was storming noisily outside of our cozy nest. "Who broke the guard chain last night? No one was on guard when I checked this morning! Good thing we didn't have a Jerry counterattack. We'd all be dead in our sacks! Rinquette, yougoo fed! You should never leave your relief until you know they are awake! You guys were just too comfortable under there."

It was the only time in my military career that I failed to fulfill my responsibility as a guard. I felt, and still do, exceptionally remorseful since Pfc. Rinquette was killed later that day when an enemy mortar round struck the roof of a house where he was taking cover.

As we crawled lethargically from our sleeping quarters and began rolling our bedrolls on the grass, a young tanker captain approached. It was Captain Melland, commander of the company to which we were attached. He took one look under the tank and turned angrily to it's driver. "If I find that camouflage net or any government property in that hole when you leave, there'll be a court-marshall" With that, he stalked off to check on the rest of his troops.

The tank crew proved to be very congenial. The crewman I remember best was the driver, a T-5 named Taylor. As we stood around waiting for orders, the mail-orderly appro-ched. "T-5 Taylor? I've a letter for you." He handed our subject a very normal looking envelope. As Taylor excitedly opened the missive, his face brightened and to our surprise, he turned a cartwheel right there in front of his tank. "Hooray! It's a boy!" he shouted, "my wife just had a baby and it's a boy!" His jubilation was contagious and soon everyone around him was shaking his hand and slapping him on the back.

As the morning dragged on, the sound of battle just over the ridge came to our ears. The characteristic burst of a burp gun sounded, too close for comfort and the rattle of returning fire was heard.

"The Seventieth is going in boys" Lt. Huff informed us. "We'll be going in behind them to take over and hold the town. Make sure everyone has rations, plenty of ammo and grenades."

As time passed, I settled into the tank's turret, at the commander's invitation, and taking out a sheet of paper and pen began to write a letter. I addressed it to my mother. As I wrote, the sounds of battle came distinctly through the air. Using the breach of the tank's cannon as a table, this would have been a classic "just before the battle, mother" letter. Realizing that the tone of my writing was too emotional and too sentimental, I tore it up and proceeded to find more constructive things to do.

Some of the tanks were moving now, and I left the turret. The semi-circle had broken up and the monstrous machines proceeded single file, over the ridge and out of sight. I never met any of our tank's crew again.

"All right, fall in. Approach march formation. We'll follow the tanks into town and take over from the Seventieth Division" said Lt. Huff. He took up his position at the head of the column and moved out at a brisk pace, leading the two dispersed columns down the road.

As we crested the hill, we saw a town below. Smoke was billowing from all quarters and the trees that lined the road showed signs that heavy artillery had very recently fallen amongst them. Saplings were cut off and giant pine trees lay where they had fallen, severed by heavy pieces of steel from the bursting shells.

The tanks were out of sight on the road ahead, except for one hapless vehicle which somehow had missed the road and gone crashing through the trees and underbrush down a precipitous hillside. The tank was hopelessly entangled in the brush and saplings which had helped to slow, and eventually stop, it's headlong plunge. The engine was roaring and the tracks moving but the monster would not move.

Soon we were at the edge of town. As we moved down a street, doughboys in roofless, windowless houses hailed us. "What outfit is this?" No answer. We had been given strict orders to not disclose our organization. We felt the order included friendly troops as well as enemy.

Up ahead, artillery was falling at a high rate. "Get your men off the street!" Lt. Huff shouted. "Take cover in doorways or anyplace where you can't be hit". A few rifle bullets snapped past. I needed no coaxing to take cover in a burned out house. The house had no roof and as I heard the whistle of incoming mortar rounds, I wished that I had chosen something more substantial. The barrage fell with deafening accuracy. Shells burst in the street and on both sides. The one with my name on it lit within three feet. Due to providential care, a two foot stone wall protected me from instant death.

The men ahead were moving again. Dashing from doorway to doorway, we made our way up the street. Mortar rounds would fall sporadically and we would take momentary cover, but no barrages such as the initial one ever fell again to slow our advance. Occasional rifle shots would keep us undercover but no known casualties were incurred, except the mortarman, Leo Rinquette. I don't know if it was during the attack, or later, that he was killed.

Lt. Huff was tossing smoke grenades in the street intersection ahead. I could see individual soldiers crossing at high port and at a full run. I noted one of our tanks parked at the corner as I passed.

My squad was to stay on the side of the street where we were, while others took up positions in doorways on the opposite side. As we dashed alternately from door to door, a fiery barrage engulfed a building across the street, but luckily about fifty feet ahead of the advancing doughboys. Black smoke followed and a string of machine gun bullets split the air to let us know that Jerry knew exactly where we were.

"Post a one man guard in that house and put the rest of your men in the cellar" Sgt. Juan ordered. "Be ready for a counterattack."

"You guys go down, I'll stand guard first," I passed the order on. German basements or "kellers" as they are known are built for situations like this. Instead of flat ceilings, they are arched. Built like a pillbox and can withstand anything but a direct hit by a shell or bomb having a delay fuze.

I whiled away my time by moving from street side to backyard, or alley side. Looking in all directions to make sure no infiltrating Krauts were coming. As I looked out the street side door, I spied what appeared to be a half-drunk civilian coming reeling down the street. A net shopping bag with two loaves of bread with tightly grasped in one hand. "Kommen sie hier" I ordered, motioning him to come closer. The offender staggered a little closer but didn't slow his march toward the enemy held buildings. Finally I raised my rifle and shouted "halt". Looking down the barrel of an M-1 Garand can be a nerve wracking experience, drunk or sober. At last he stopped. "Vas haben sie?" I asked. "Nicht ferstehn" was the answer as he nervously eyed the gun with which I now was probing his shopping bag. "Wo gehen sie?" I asked. "Nicht ferstehn", again his stock reply. Uncertainly, he staggered on down the street toward the enemy lines. I drew a bead between his shoulder blades as he went. "Heck", I thought, "I can't do that. I refuse to shoot anyone in the back". A bullet from the enemy position smacked the air, and the man flinched. His knees bent, but he didn't go down and continued steadfastly down the street with all the information the enemy needed to make our lives miserable for the next two days.

The drunk hadn't been gone a half hour before I heard the ominous rush of an incoming mortar barrage. I should have known better, but instead of falling prone to the floor, I thought I had time to make it to the cellar. I met the barrage at an open window that faced the backyard. As round after round exploded with deafening effect. I felt that the whole house was coming down around me. "Oh Oh, I'm hit" I thought as I felt a sharp pain in the fingers of my left hand. As the explosions subsided and the air in the room cleared, I looked at my hand. Instead of a bloody stump, as I expected, all I saw was a white powdery deposit where a piece of plaster from the wall had impacted. The button from the left sleeve was missing and I was feeling very fortunate to be alive. A few minutes later, as I was looking for the enemy assault that was eminately expected, I checked the working of my M-1 rifle. To my horror, I couldn't open the bolt. Panic set in as I struggled to open the breech. "What if the counterattack comes now?" I asked myself. "It usually comes on the heels of an artillery barrage such as we have just experienced. I have only one round to fire, I've got to get another rifle."

Morosely, I went to the cellar door and shouted to the guys seated on the floor around a candle that flickered weakly on a box they had found. "Chandler, take over for me, my rifle got hit in that barrage. I'm going back up the street and see if the crew of that tank at the corner might have one I can trade for." Reluctantly, Frank picked up his rifle and came deliberately up the stairs. After briefing him on the situation, I made a dash into the street. Running half bent over, I made it to the second doorway. It takes three seconds to draw a bead on any target with any accuracy and I figured I gave any Kraut that might be watching, a lot more than that before I came to safety in the doorway.

The house was empty, so I proceeded to go through it and out the back door into the backyard. Leaping over a couple of fences, I figured that it was time to take cover in the next house, which I did. Passing through the building as I had done before, I was once again on the street. Bending low, I made a final dash to where the tank was sitting. I'll never know why, but the tank was completely buttoned up. Perhaps the crew was concerned with flying shrapnel, or were just keeping warm, but they certainly left themselves vulnerable to an attacking German bazooka.

With the butt of my rifle pounding on the turret, I made my presence known to the reticent crew. The hatch opened slowly and the commander's head emerged. "Ya, whatcha want?" he asked. "I was wondering if you guys might have a spare M-1. Mine just got hit and I can't open the bolt" I responded. "We just happen to have one, picked it up from a wounded Dough about a week ago. It only shoots single shot though. We carried it on the outside of our tank for quite awhile and it got wet."

"I'll take it, I almost begged, anything is better than what I have. It's only good for one shot and we're expecting a counter attack any minute."

As we made the exchange, I lingered a few moments standing on the tank, making small talk with the commander. The black-top street suddenly erupted with the force of a monstrous artillery shell that plowed a furrow the width of the street. We heard the "pop" of its fuze and watched as the ponderous projectile came to rest at the base of a tree not thirty yards away. The lethal missile lay there on the ground with its fuze smoking. Thank God for duds!! The enemy knew exactly where I was and had to have perfect vision in order to fire a flat trajectory gun and place a round with such deadly accuracy. The only thing he hadn't known was that this round would never explode. Once more, my God saw fit to spare me.

Loosing my hand hold on the tank, I slid quickly to the ground. At full speed, I ran to the corner and made my way, door to door until I reached our assigned stronghold.

Lt. Huff was in the front room and the rest of the squad were milling around, taking furtive glances out the windows to assure that no attack was forth coming.

"McGill, I want you to take your men and check out that row of houses by the railroad", ordered Lt. Huff. "I don't think you'll find any Krauts, but set up and outpost and watch for any activity across the tracks. Jerry seems to have left everything on this side for us. Keep your men in the cellar and post a one man guard." "Yes Sir," was my reply. "You guys heard Huff, get your stuff and lets go!"

There was a vacant area between our street and the row of houses that we were to occupy. As we prepared to cross the open space, I told the men, "Follow me, one at a time. Don't anyone start until the other reaches the objective. Keep low and double time." Away I went not knowing if the buildings were enemy occupied or not. Bent low and zig-zagging, I made it with no incident. Waving the next man across, each of the four, made it safely. Kitchen had barely clear the opening, when the whole area was engulfed with a deadly mortar barrage. Another indication that the enemy had perfect observation our activities. Had there been another man in our squad, he would, doubt have been caught squarely in the barrage.

Safely inside the first house, he began to check it for any unwanted occupants. The upper floors were clear, so we proceeded to the cell coming down the dimly lit stairway, we were aware of muffled voices in the room below. Cautiously opening a door, we came on a room lit by candlelight with two men and a woman huddled around a table in one corner. "Wo ist der Deutsch soldat?" I asked. "Nicht soldat, nicht kine soldat." One of the men replied. At that very moment a tremendous explosion rocked the entire house. Dust fell from the ceiling and the candle flickered. A very large caliber artillery shell had just exploded inches from the foundation of the house. The poor civilians were more shaken than we. What sudden destruction had these irresponsible Americans brought us?

A quick look outside revealed a large shell crater and the fact that this was not a basement at all, but what we would call a "walk-out."

"Let's get out of here," I said. "I want a house with a safe basement. Cover me while I see what those other houses are like." To the south of this row of dwellings, ran a railroad, parallel to the street. Apparently Lt. Huff's assumption was true. The enemy had left this side and was now busily preparing to defend the south side of the tracks and to place harassing fire on us. For the later, I would say he was doing an outstanding job. The next building was what I considered a duplex with a basement and two levels of living space on either side of a stone masonry partition. There was a connecting opening in the basement, or rather cellar. (both sides had the arched roofs that we needed for best safety.) The apartment on the side facing the enemy was unoccupied but the "friendly" side housed a mature woman, a grandmotherly type and two teen age girls. "This is the place," I said. "We'll keep a man on guard on the side facing the enemy, while the rest take up living in the keller."

The girls seemed friendly enough. We fraternized some, sharing our chocolate bars, coffee and hard candy. We even played a game of checkers. Their rules were quite different from ours and much to their glee, they were able to beat us each time. As darkness fell, to our surprise the girls disappeared. No doubt due to the wisdom of the two older women.

As we settled in for the night, Chandler and I thought we would do a bit of midnight reconnaissance to find out if there was any food or other refreshments available in the friendly side. As we crawled throu the opening between the two kellers, our flashlight beam fell on a bed in one end of the room. Grandma, with her nightgown and headset was sitting upright in the bed, her toothless mouth was open and she looked every bit like the goblins we used to portray on Halloween. End of the excursion. We almost got stuck in the opening as we both tried to exit at the same time. Needless to say, we didn't stray from our chosen sanctuary for the rest of the night.

Morning broke after an uneventful night. When we came up the stairs on the "friendly" side, we were shocked to find one of the girls in the arms of a young man. "Das ist mine dalink," the young man asserted. Not to our liking at all!! What was this army age fellow doing in this house, making love to the girls that we thought might be our best friends?"

After questioning the stray young man in our halting German, we found that he was AWOL from the German army, and that he had found his way across Germany from the Eastern Front, just to reach his home town as the Americans moved in. "Chandler, hustle this guy up to the C. P., Captain Powers will know how to deal with him." We were all glad to see our competition removed.

Our joy was short lived, however, as Lt. Huff appeared on the scene. After the formalities were over, he ordered us to move up the street to another building, similar to the one we were in, so that we would be in a better position to prevent any enemy infiltration. The new quarters were much the same as those we just left except that the "friendly" side was occupied by a couple, the wife was very obviously pregnant. It looked as though delivery could begin at any time. The family was cordial enough, and we gained access to the vacant enemy side through the two foot square opening in the wall in the keller.

Sometime during the afternoon, someone spied two German soldiers sitting on the edge of their foxhole. They were shirtless and were soaking in the rays of the springtime sunshine. Lt. Huff was on the scene and immediately got on the walkie talkie radio. "Send Sgt. Anderson (our company radioman) to our position in the row of buildings alongside the railroad." We weren't sure who he was talking to, but a breathless Sgt. Anderson soon arrived. With crisp instructions, giving co-ordinates to an unknown artillery battery, he soon told us, "the rounds are on their way." With a mighty rush the projectiles whistled overheard and crashed loudly in the area where the Krauts had been seen. No more evidence of enemy presence was seen.

"You guys stay where you are," Sgt. Huff ordered, "I'm going to have Sgt. McBride set up his machine guns in the last house in this row. With that he departed. Sometime later, as dusk fell over the lands. Chandler and I decided to take a walk and see how the machine gun detail was going to protect our flank. We walked brazenly, and I must say quite ignorantly, down the sidewalk between the buildings and the railroad, past the house where one of the machine-guns was supposed to be set-up in an upper room with a gapping shell hole. No one challenged us and we walked right in the backdoor. The second floor room was full of troops, all seemingly without leadership. They were all milling around not sure what they were supposed to do. "Who's in charge here?" I shouted, "You guys could all be dead. We walked right past your gun and nobody challenged us." I was a bit ticked and perhaps feeling a little bravado. "What's the matter, McGill? I'm in charge." Lt. Huff came out of the gloom. "We're trying to get detail organized. You better get back to your men." "Don't you know that a Jerry patrol could have wiped out your whole operation here ??? asked," (I loved pulling Huff's chain.)

That night, around ten or eleven o'clock, the artificial moon-light was turned off. This was created by a series of flood lights that aimed at the clouds and were designed to cut down on enemy patrols to aid the movement of our forces. Soon the air-raid sirens in Sarrbruken began to wail, Sarrbruken is just a few kilometers from our ???istion. The sound of many aircraft followed as flight after flight American bombers passed overhead, headed toward targets deep inside ??? many. It was an eerie yet heartwarming experience.

The night passed quietly enough. Along about mid-morning, I decided to take a little walk by myself. The enemy artillery that had been so active and so accurate the first day of our occupation, was now quite subdued. We felt quite safe moving about as long as we kept the row of houses between us and the enemy. I moved back into town where I found evidence of the extensive work that the enemy had gone to to defend this portion of their turf. Anti-tank traps had been dug between houses to prevent the entrance of armor, and on one street I came on a large pillbox facing the opposite direction from which the seventieth division, and eventually the Twelfth Armored entered the town. I had picked up an unused Panzerfaust, (German bazooka) on my way and now determined that I would try it out on the pillbox. At a range of about thirty feet from the pillbox was a zig-zag communications trench. From this position, I planned to fire the weapon. I reasoned that since this was a rocket, I could fire and duck to the protection of the trench before it exploded. Wrong! The shock of the explosion knocked me down and literally shovelsfull of dirt fell on me. Surprised, I stood up and brushed the dirt from my uniform and from my weapon. Peering into the pillbox, I spied a menacing looking water cooled machine-gun mounted on a platform with it's muzzle pointing in the direction from which I had just come. The pillbox was empty of personnel, but the gun was fully loaded with a fresh belt of ammunition and appeared not to have been fired. Once more my luck held and I foolishly found myself in a position where I had no business to be.

Late that afternoon, the man on guard in our observation position, called down the stairway to the rest of the squad in the keller: "Something's happening! I think the Krauts are attacking." I made my way quickly up the stairs and peered out the window toward the far side of the railroad track. The area was filled with smoke, and as we watched additional shells fell, spreading more smoke canisters. At that point, Lt. Huff appeared on the scene. "You better have your men pull back to the other side of the house. I don't want anyone trapped on this side if those guys get across that railroad track." We had all been prepared to hold our position if the enemy did come, but the order to pull back was welcome anyway. Down the stairs to the keller we went. "Okay you guys let's get back on the otherside. Huff thinks the Krauts are going to attack us and he doesn't want us to get trapped. By now the excitement had grown, and as we passed one by one thru the hole in the wall I expected to have a grenade thrown down our stairway by an attacker at any moment. Finally it was my turn to crawl though. I struggled to do so, but with my ammunition belt, canteen, bayonet and first aid pack, I was just too big to make it. Nervously I backed up and removing my cartridge belt with all it's attachments crawled thru, pulling the offending equipment after me. In the street outside, the men were waiting. "Better hold up right here." Huff said. "You'll have to keep someone in a position to watch the other side. You'll have to figure out how you want to do that." With that he walked off to see how the rest of his platoon was doing. Well this called for a little ingenuity. I didn't want to have anyone go back down in the keller and up the other side to watch the enemy, and I certainly didn't want anyone to walk around the building in plain sight of him. "We'll have to punch a hole in the wall that separates the two apartments," I reasoned. Laying our bazooka on the window ledge, I aimed at the opposite wall and pulled the trigger. When the dust cleared, I could see that only a little plaster had been removed from the foot thick masonry wall. Climbing in the window, I set a concussion type grenade in the largest space that I could find between the stones. I pulled the pin and jumped out the window. With a deafening crash, the grenade exploded, sending rock particles and throughout the room. By the two explosions, the rocks had been suffi??? loosened that with our entrenching tools and a lot of prying and pou???ing, we soon had an opening that a fully clothed and equipped man co??? comfortably pass through.

At this point, the man of the house and his pregnant wife emerged from the keller. Blinking from the unacustomed light, the man looked in??? may at the rubble pile and dust encrusted furniture. His eyes fell on the hole in the wall. "Artillery?" he asked. "No," he answered his own question. He looked at the open window and then turned to me??? with a accusing look. I guess he realized that we were not playing games, and that the hole was a necessity brought on by the dangerous situation that we had been placed in. At any rate, he and his wife tired once more to the keller.

We were standing in the street, awaiting any new developments from ??? sentry on the other side of the wall when Lt. Huff returned. "I guess it wasn't a counter attack after all. The Seventieth Division just took control of the other side of the tracks and we are to be relieved tonight. Be ready to move your men to the CP as soon as it gets da???

It was with great relief that we left our positions and moved to the center of town where we met the rest of the company and our commander Capt. Powers. "We'll move in two columns, by platoons. We are going to the town of Forbach, about ten or twelve kilometers from here keep the men dispersed as we expect some artillery fire as we cross the mountain." The road march was orderly and without incident until we reached the outskirts of Forbach. At that point all hell broke out the road we had just taken. Artillery barrage after barage fell. I hope no other troops were following us as they certainly would have suffered heavy casualties from the terrific bombardment.

Finding a vacant house, we prepared to spend the night and get some rest. Chandler and I took charge of a room with a bed but no mattress only bare springs. We at least didn't have to sleep on the floor as some of our comarades were forced to do. As we took off our cartridge belts and prepared to use them for pillows. Chandler decided to check his grenades. "Hey McGill, look at this one. The cotter pin is just hanging on by the tip of one leg. There would have been an awful mess to clean up in the morning if the pin fell out!" The hazards of war aren't all due to enemy action!

Chapter VI

DRIVE TO THE RHINE & BEYOND

The cold winds and snow of late winter in the Alsatian Province had given way to more kindly, warmer springlike weather. It was mid–March and the farmers were loading manure, from the winters collection, onto their wagons and transporting it to their fields. Here it was being spread carefully to provide the needed nutrients for next summers crop. The aromatic manure piles were usually located near the front door of each home in the little country village of Trittling, where we had been billeted for about two weeks.

Ever since the experience of Sterling-Wendel, we had been stationed in this small village. We were in Seventh Army reserve and had been training in the art of pillbox warfare with anticipation of assaulting the Siegfried Line. In the immediate area there were several abandoned pillboxes, a part of the now defunct Maginot Line. These offered a variety of targets for training the troops in the finer points of overcoming enemy that had decided to defend their home turf from the security of concrete bunkers.

We had been fortunate to find housing with an elderly couple who lived in a classic example of the Alsatian home. The building not only housed the family living quarters, but also the barn for the livestock. There was adequate storage for hay and grain for feeding the cattle, chickens and geese which co-habited with the people. During inclement weather there was no need for the farmer to go out into the snow and cold as everything was conveniently located under the same roof.

When we were first ordered to find housing for the squad, I knocked on the door. The husband answered. He was probably in his sixties and quite friendly. Apparently the Burgomeister had forewarned his people that they might be called on to house some of their liberators. I'm not sure that everyone appreciated our presence in their village, but no one dared to let on that we were not welcome. During the past, this portion of Europe had been subjected to French rule several times, but had often reverted to German lordship. Right now, everyone spoke German and when asked their nationality said that they were "Alsatian".

The door opened to an inviting living room. In the corner stood the largest, most ornate space heater I had ever seen. The outside of the stove was covered with a glazed ceramic tile, bright green in color. Thru the icing-glass openings in the heaters door, we could see a cheery fire burning. The wife, dressed all in black, was sitting at a table reading her Bible. This was a shock for me as I had heard that Hitler had banned all manner of religious activity, and that church attendance since he and his Nazi party came into power was taboo. With my limited command of the German language, I let him know that we needed a place for our squad to stay while in their town. We were told that we could use the living room, much to our pleasure. It didn't take long for the twelve man squad to get situated. With some of our chocolate bars and "K" ration coffee, we soon made friends with the home owners. Sitting around the kitchen table, in the evening, we would share our rations in exchange for their limited store of good German bread and butter.

To our pleasant surprise, we were introduced to two nieces that had moved to the village from the city to avoid the danger of American bombs. These young ladies had come to live with their relatives for the duration. The youngest, Marie Therese, was sixteen. An attractive, blonde, rosy cheeked "madchen". She was quite friendly but very shy, with a tendency for her face to turn rosy red whenever any of us tried to talk to her. She made it a habit of attending daily evening vespers in their church nearby. One evening, as I was returning from getting something from our half-track, I happened to spot her returning from church. I fell in step with her, intending to escort her to the house and make some small talk. I had barely finished "Gute Abend", when she bent her head, pulled her scarf over her face, and with a giggle, took off on a run for the front door of their home.

Our days were spent in the field, usually with problems involving pillboxes. One particular problem involved making a "Pole Charge" and simulating an attack on a pillbox. The pole charge was nothing other than a bunch of nitro-starch blocks tied to a long pole which could be leaned against an embrasure of a pillbox and the fuze lighted. The charge was supposed to be large enough that the concussion from its' explosion would kill or neutralize all occupants. For this particular exercise, I found a nice long slender sapling and very carefully removed the bark. After the problem was finished, the umpire called for a critique. The tankers and riflemen gathered around to hear what he had to say. "The attack went off according to plan", he said, "I could hardly see the troops, but I could see that bright pole with the charge on it coming thru the woods a mile away. I would suggest that in the future a pole be chosen that will blend with the background."

The point was well taken. I felt somewhat embarrassed that I had chosen to use a pole that was devoid of all natural camouflage. My embarrassment over the bright pole was nothing compared to what I experienced later when Captain Powers asked if anyone in the company knew how to set off the charge and I volunteered. I had had explosives training in my basic with the Combat Engineers in Camp Abbot, Oregon. I felt that I could detonate the charge by unscrewing the fuze from a fragmentation grenade and inserting it into the hole in a block of Nitro-starch. In theory, it should have worked as it was a good fit. Someone in the crowd had a large ball of twine with which to remotely pull the pin on the grenade detonator. With the pole charge in place and the twine tied to the grenade pin, I played out about fifty yards of twine and took cover in the zig-zag trench in front of the pillbox. The Infantry were standing behind the tanks and cautiously peeking around them to see what was happening. I gave a healthy pull on the twine. Nothing happened. I pulled again with greater enthusiasm. The pole charge separated from the pillbox and came tumbling down into the trench. Thankfully the trench was dug zig-zag so that an explosion in one area would not directly involve people in other parts of the trench. I'm sure a lesson learned by the Germans the hard way. I was thankful for their thoughtfulness. Still no explosion and no sound of a detonator activating. After a short wait to be assured that the charge was not going to go off, I cautiously approached it. There lying in the bottom of the trench was the charge, with the fuze still in place. The cotter key that held the fuze safe was barely engaged, in fact it looked like it could fall out at any moment. The twine was still attached, so signalling to my audience to stay where they were, I returned to my position further down the trench and with a mighty yank pulled the cotter key free of it's position. There was an audible "Pop," as the detonator for the timing charge ignited. After the normal delay time on the grenade fuze another louder "Splut" was heard. No explosion? This can't be!! Running up to where the charge lay in the trench, I viewed my folly. The block which had contained the fuze, had now completely disintegrated. The initiating charge had not been large enough to create the explosion that I expected. I'm sure there was a lot of sighs of relief from the observers. None of us knew just how lethal an explosion could be expected of a charge this big and it could have resulted in some serious injuries had the charge indeed exploded. Captain Powers seemed relieved as well as he ordered the non-coms to road march their troops back to their billets.

"Birtch, get ahold of Sgt. Winters. He has some O. D. paint. We have orders to paint out all vehicular identification." Lt. Huff was standing in the doorway of our cozy quarters. "You guys will have to remove all shoulder patches and turn them in to the C.P. Get rid of all your letters that show our address. We're going to the Third Army to help old Blood-n-guts, Patton move his army to the Rhine. Not sure when we'll jump off, but be ready to move within an hours notice." Since our regular half-track driver, Sigismund Ryfinski had drawn the winning number to go on pass to Brussels, Pfc. Birtch had been acting in his place.

It was an early morning hour and as yet no training schedule for the day had been issued. We busied ourselves with collecting our meager possessions and stowing them, along with our bedrolls in the half-track. About mid-morning, our platoon Sgt. Bernie Manion appeared with instructions to be mounted up and ready to depart at 1200 hours.

Since we had been in Seventh Army reserve for about two weeks, we had been issued regular civilian type brooms to keep our quarters tidy. We had immediately made the broom available to the lady of the house. We might as well have given her an expensive vacuum cleaner. The broom hardly was idle from morning till night. The standard type broom used in this corner of the world was a bundle of willow twigs lashed to a crude branch. Needless to say the performance of such a tool was not too efficient. Our hostess was enamored with our broom and when I told her that it was U. S. Army property and that I had to take it with me or suffer the consequences, she broke down in tears. I still wonder at the hardness of my heart in those days.

Well, the order to "Mount up" came. The half-track, with it's motor idling, was in front of the building with the men climbing in and finding their places. I was standing in the door of our billet saying good-bye to our hosts when a tearful Marie Therese came up. I tenderly put my arm around her and asked her for a kiss. She complied and I felt like I was leaving a very good friend behind. This was the extent of my romantic involvement during our service in Europe. I hope that she found happiness with someone who spoke her language and would make a happy life for her.

The average speed of an armored column in transit is fifteen miles per hour. I don't know how far it is from our billets near St. Avold to the city of Trier, but it was mid-day, after an all night motor march, when we approached the city. The only significant thing that I recall about this place is the immense Bailey bridge erected by Army Engineers to see us safely across a river that ran in a very deep gorge. Having some experience with Bailey bridges during my basic training, I was awed by the tremendous accomplishment of the Engineers who had been there long before we arrived.

The plan, as explained to us by Lt. Huff, was for the Armor to overtake the spearheading Infantry, (I believe it was the 99th Division) and take over the assault. Well it took two days before we were able to say that we were really in the lead. The Infantry had been moving rapidly, with only slight opposition. They were being transported by truck whenever the situation allowed rapid movement.

As we moved across country, our lead elements, the point, would often run into ambushes and frequently suffer loss. We came on a scout jeep burning one evening and were held up while the task force commander ordered the dozer tank forward. The tank lowered its blade and unceremoniously pushed the offending Jeep over the mountain side, where it continued to burn as the task force moved on.

Another similar incident occurred the next evening when the task force was halted and the Infantry ordered to dismount. We were told to disperse in the woods to the right of the road and to clear all enemy troops that we might encounter. We had not gone more than a hundred yards when we saw a stalled Jeep on the road. The windshield was laced by a string of machine-gun bullets and the occupants were no-where to be seen. The tanks were creeping along the road, keeping pace with us, when I heard a tanker scream at the top of his voice, "Here they come!! Get this thing out of here!!" Two loud explosions were heard as Panzerfaust exploded against the first tank. The sound of small arms fire filled the air as every rifle in our assault group was discharged into the woods across the road. In the dusk of the woods I almost stepped on a German Soldier. He had lain silent while the lead squads of our company passed by, but somehow my path lead directly to the spot where he lay. In an instant, he was on his feet and running toward the road. I lowered my rifle on him. I didn't shoot because I realized that he had a large red cross on his back. Obviously a Medic. On his way to the road, a buddy joined him. He also wore the red cross. I kept my sights on the two as they emerged from the woods onto the road and walked bravely toward the task force, and surrender. By this time the firing had ceased and no more enemy action was forthcoming. The tank that was hit was still able to keep up with the convoy so the anti-tank fire must not have hit a sensitive spot.

The next day our task force was halted in a small town. Whenever there was houses on either side of the street, the danger of snipers was always a concern. "Looks like we'll be here awhile," Lt. Huff said. "Have your men dismount and clean out these houses. We don't want any trigger happy snipers taking us by surprise."

Our squad entered the first convenient house and made a thorough search of the basement and lower level. As I climbed the stairway to the attic, I was alone. The others had found other things to pay attention to, like a kitchen stocked with eggs and potatoes. Some of us actually knew how to make American Fries and cook eggs. A window in an attic gable stood open and as I looked out onto the roof I saw what looked like fresh mud from a shoe or boot on the shingles. "That's funny," I mused. "Looks like someone came in here quite recently." Without further thought I continued my search for hidden enemy soldiers. I spied a bedroom with a tremendous large bed with a bulging feather tick. The tick was spotless white and filled with down. It billowed and beckoned for me to try it. I said to myself, "Mom would never let me do this, but she's not here so here goes." With full gear, rifle, helmet, ammo belt, bayonet and canteen, I took a running jump and landed smack in the middle of the feather tick. My muddy combat boots left their imprint, but the shear pleasure of jumping up and down on such a beautiful bed was unimaginable. When the jumping was finished, I lay down for a peaceful rest on the first bed I'd seen in a week. I was just beginning to become drowsy when I heard a disturbance in the hall. Here was Dentino and Morino without helmets or weapons with a German soldier by the scurf of the neck. The scurf of the neck was not a good description, because he was wearing only the long sleeved underwear issued by the Wermacht. The bottom part of his body was fully clothed, with uniform trousers and boots. "We found this guy in bed in one of the rooms that we thought we had checked. The room had two doors and we thought we had already been in there," said Dentino. "He had taken his tunic off and hidden it under the bed. We were going thru the dresser drawers looking for weapons when Moreno saw him. He just punched me and said,' Shouldn't we do something about him?' We don't have our weapons, would you take him down and head him toward the rear? Our Second and Anti-tank platoons are supposed to be back there somewhere collecting our prisoners."

Unceremoniously I punched the prisoner with the muzzle of my rifle and muttered "Rouse." He understood and we walked down the stairs out into the street. The prisoner was numbed by the sight of so many tanks and half-tracks. He just stood for a moment, not knowing what to do until I fired my rifle in the air and pointed in the direction that I wanted him to go. His knees half buckled at the report of my M-1, but he got the idea that he was to "Mach schnell" in the direction that I had indicated. Amid hoots and hollers from the watching tankers, he took off at a good pace down the line without blouse or helmet. I'm sure he was well treated by his captors.

Outside another village, we were told to dismount and proceed into town on foot. Apparently there was some opposition up ahead and it would be unwise to go barreling into town without properly securing it first. As we waited for the order to proceed, a bullet clipped a branch over my head warning me that this one might not be as easy as most towns had been in the past few days. Smoke from burning buildings was evident up ahead and as we entered the town, the body of a German soldier lay across our path. Some marksman had put him down as he apparently tried to abandon his post and run to the rear.

All went well as we proceeded, in two columns, up the main street toward the town center where several buildings were well enveloped in flames. As I crossed a street, a fire hose was stretched out in it and as I came abreast of the nozzle, someone opened the fire hydrant and the hose started to flail about without anyone on the business end. A group of civilians had gathered across from the flaming building and as a man picked up the nozzle and directed the stream at me, they all began to laugh and cheer. I leveled my rifle on the offending fireman and the cheering stopped. The whole crowd mysteriously dissolved until only a few brave souls remained. I could see the humor in the situation and had no serious intention to harm any of the townspeople. I lowered my rifle and continued with the rest of the platoon to make certain that no enemy stragglers remained in town.

As I lay on my stomach, at the corner of a church, I was astonished to see a priest in full ecclesiastical gown and head-gear approach and go calmly about his business. When I tried to warn him to go back, he merely shrugged his shoulders and said something like, "Kreige ist nicht gute." I guess he had higher goals.

Well, we were through the town, and to my knowledge no one even fired his rifle. The half-racks came up and we proceeded to mount up and join the tanks as the task force once more moved out of town and on up the side of a steep forested hill. We had not gone far when we realized that this road and woods had been used to hide an enemy ammunition dump. About every hundred feet was a stack of artillery shells. To each and every stack was a light green electric wire. Our column was topped right in the midst of this booby trap. Sweat must have come on the brows of most of our people as we saw where one stack had detonated and mowed down trees for at least a hundred feet in all directions. We were told later that the detonating source had been disconnected and that the area was perfectly safe. Perfectly safe? I don't think so.

Apparently the task force was not moving fast enough for old Blood and Guts, so the order came down to forget about the slow careful approach to taking this country, let's go through the towns with guns blazing and keep the enemy pinned down so he won't want to show himself. The Infantry would come behind us and clean up the bypassed troops. This was kind of fun, as some of us hadn't fired a shot since the advance began. When we came to a town, all machine-guns and rifles would fire at will. Usually we would shoot out windows or street lights. I saw some good marksmanship exhibited by Pvt. Allen Bark. With the drivers sub-machine gun, he would "plink" out street lights with impressive accuracy. We didn't know that he was that good a shot. As we passed though a village, I was having a ball shooting out plate glass windows. As I was about to add another to my list I realized that there was someone behind it. Looking closer, I realized that it was an old lady with a white handkerchief in her hand. She was waving frantically and grinning as if she was overjoyed to see the end of the war coming. How tragic it would have been if I had not held my fire.

Our rations had mostly been of the official "K" variety, unless we were fortunate enough to stop temporarily in a town where we would take over a house and cook a meal of potatoes and eggs. In one particular town we entered a home, uninvited, and told the woman and young children to leave. The woman promptly got rid of the children but refused to leave her cherished kitchen regardless of our threats and orders. She was one determined Hausfrau. I'll always respect he for that. She realized that all we really wanted was a home cooked meal, and in her German language gave us to know that she was not leaving her home for anyone, and that she would do the cooking. She did a good job, and when we had finished eating, we thanked her and went our way. I don't think we made any friends that day, but we learned how tough a woman who loved her home and family can be.

The next day we were halted in another town. Out of nowhere, Lt. Hune, the first platoon leader, appeared and informed us that there was trouble up ahead. He ordered us to clear all houses of potential snipers while we waited for things to clear up. As I finished going though the nearest building from bottom to top, I happened to look out an attic window. There to my surprise, less than a kilometer away were two knocked out Sherman tanks. One was belching black smoke, the other sat motionless as well. A group of men was proceeding up a slight knoll. It was obvious that they were the crews of the tanks with their captors following. On the crest of the knoll were two dug in anti-tank guns. The guns must have been placed hurriedly. No attempt to camouflage or hide them had been made. They were sitting right out in plain sight, from our position, and the point tanks of our task force had blundered right into them.

Removing my helmet to avoid giving notice to any observing riflemen, I stuck my head out the window and called to S/Sgt. Juan in the street below. "Come on up here, I've a perfect view of an enemy anti-tank battery". Hastily, Juan, with Lt. Hune in tow came stumbling up the stairs.

As we watched with fascination, suddenly the stonework around the window began to fragment as dozens of bullets impacted with a strange "Pinging" sound. The plaster behind us began to fly off the wall in little puffs as the bullets from an unseen machine-gun flew by our heads. By some miracle, none of us was hit. I believe in Devine Providence and I'm sure that God was with us that day. We had been foolish enough to expose ourselves to the enemy and almost paid a terrible price for our mistake.

Coming back down to our vehicle, we found a somewhat shaken, but smiling Pfc. Birtch. Proudly he displayed a captured P-38 pistol, the prize collectors item of every American Infantryman. "I was cleaning out the half-track, when someone touched me on the arm," he related, "when I turned around, here was this German soldier standing and pointing to the pistol in his holster. He wanted to give up real bad and I obliged by taking his pistol and heading him toward the back end of the column. I was pretty shook."

I'm not sure how the opposition from the anti-tank guns was overcome, but it was not too long before the order to mount up was given and the column began to move again. At the end of the street our route made a sharpe turn to the left and we saw the body of an American soldier lying on a stretcher, covered by a G. I. blanket. On top of the body was the soldiers helmet with two silver bars. This war was no respecter of rank. Our junior officers paid a high price for their positions of authority.

Our original objective, according to Lt. Huff, was Mannheim, a city on the Rhine river. Today our objective has changed and we are now to proceed to the city of Ludwigshaven. Didn't make much difference to us, but the road to Ludwigshaven was a four lane freeway, the first "Autobahn" that we had seen. It offered much better traveling than the other route.

"First Squad, you'll be in the point," ordered our platoon leader, "They said we had to furnish one squad and it might as well be you. You'll have two tanks ahead of you and you will be about a mile ahead of the task force. You better start right away, the tanks are waiting for you up on the Autobahn. Cpl. Ford has a BAR (Browning Automatic Rifle), I don't know where he got it, but you'll need all the fire power you can get so he said you could use it." I had never fired a BAR in all my military career, but I knew of its reputation so I gladly traded my trusted M-1 for Cpl. Fords' BAR. Pfc. Birtch was in the drivers seat, S/Sgt. Juan was on the fifty caliber machine-gun. I was in charge of the SCR-300 radio with which I was to relay any information to the task force commander. With my trusty BAR and radio, I snuggled up tight to the front of the passenger compartment. Pvt. Bark was next to me with the drivers sub-machine gun, Ganyard, Ell, Kitchen, Drozd and Chandler occupied the remaining seats.

As we pulled up on the Autobahn, Pfc. Ganyard exclaimed, "Man, this is just like home in Ohio," "Might be," I returned, "but I have a bad feeling about this assignment. Someone is going to get hurt. I don't think it will be me, but someone is going to 'get it'." I still marvel at the accuracy of that prediction.

Things went along very nicely for about three or four miles when all at once we saw the two tanks ahead of us make a 180 degree turn and head back toward the task force in the other lane. Ahead of us was the rubble of a blown bridge or overpass and in the field beside the approach were several foxholes. As our vehicle began it's turn, Sgt. Juan opened up on the foxholes with the fifty caliber machine-gun. Simultaneously, I began to fire the BAR and everyone else his weapon. Something heavy smacked the built up armor plate of the the machine-gun turret. Sparks flew in front of my face. Several more explosions were heard. With each new explosion I would pull back a little further and continue to squeeze the trigger. Tracer bullets were streaming from the outskirts of a village on a hill about a mile to the north of our position. Shouts of "I'm hit," were heard and I had the impression of a pillow filled with many small holes in front of me. I believe now that it was the back of Allen Barks field jacket that was shredded by tiny pieces of shrapnel. The engine quit. The vehicle was midway between the two lanes, on the grass of the median. I could still see tracer bullets coming from the village. We had obviously been hit by a 20 millimeter anti-aircraft gun.

Everyone was bailing out of the stalled vehicle. I saw Kitchen roll very carefully over the edge of the track. I later remarked that was the only time I ever saw him take appropriate precautions when facing the enemy. I remember seeing Pfc. Birtch's face, covered with blood. A shell had exploded between the frontal armor plate and the glass windshield, filling his forehead with tiny splinters of glass or steel. Thankfully, he could still see. I exited the vehicle standing up. As I hit the concrete roadway, my left leg buckled and my knee struck the pavement with a paralyzing impact. No time to stand and feel the pain. As we ran down the embankment to the field, we had the roadway between us and the entrenched infantry and the anti-aircraft gun.

I caught up to S/Sgt Juan, whose arm was bleeding profusely. His neck had severe cuts as well and a white piece of what I assumed was tendon was exposed. "Do you think I'll make Z. I.?" He grinned. Z. I. was the term that G. I's used to designate the USA. or the Zone of Interior. "You won't if we don't stop that arm from bleeding," I answered. Taking off my belt, I placed it around his upper arm and tightened it firmly. All this time we were steadily putting distance between us and the abandoned half-track "Where's Bark?" I asked after taking inventory of the running soldiers around me. "Oh he's dead. He just got a silly look on his face and crumbled over on the floor." Kitchen volunteered. I hadn't been aware of his body when leaving the half-track. I must have stepped right over him in the confusion and not seen him.

"My leg hurts," Pfc. Ell complained as we came to a cross-road and slowed to a walk. "Drop your trousers and let me see," I ordered. As I checked over his leg, I saw a small bloody hole where a bit of shrapnel had entered the back of his thigh. Conveniently, a Medic jeep, with Red-cross flying came down the road. The jeep had 99th division identification, but it stopped at our hand signal. "Give me your rifle, you're going to the hospital," I told him. I had left the BAR in the half-track and at this point I was weaponless deep in enemy territory. I wondered how I was going to explain that predicament. T/5 Ford was furious when he learned the fate of his treasured BAR.

At this point an impeccably dressed German officer came trotting down the road with his hands laced behind his head. He was smiling and turning his head from side to side to make sure everyone knew he meant no harm. I had vowed that I would shoot the first German I saw. With my newly acquired rifle I moved menacingly toward him, hoping that someone would stop me before I made good on my promise. I'm thankful that someone grabbed the barrel of my rifle and deflected it while someone else grabbed my arm. In a situation like this rational thinking isn't always the rule and I was emotionally upset. There was one dead and three wounded, two seriously.

From our vantage point back with the task force, we could still see our half-track sitting on the Autobahn. German soldiers were all over it, no doubt taking any rations or souvenirs that they found. I lost a pistol that Chandler had given me as well as a store of chocolate bars and cigarettes that I was hoarding for barter when we were once more in a quiet situation.

Several days later I was asked by First Seargent Berry if I knew what happened to Dale Ell. "We've got him listed as missing in action," he said. "Oh, I put him on a 99ᵗʰ Division Jeep and sent him back to a hospital. He had shrapnel in his leg." was my reply. I was happy to learn that he and Pfc. Birtch were both returned to the company before the division was disbanded.

With S/Sgt. Juan wounded and evacuated, I was now the titular squad leader. I had no vehicle and only five men to lead. "You'll be my platoon runner," Lt. Huff told me. "You can ride with the mortar squad and your men will be divided up between the machine-gun squad and the other two Infantry squads. I want you to help me keep the squad leaders informed of my orders and let me know where they are at all times." This was an easy assignment for me as Lt. Huff generally knew what everyone under his command was doing. I more or less was now a free agent.

The next day we were on the outskirts of Ludwigshaven. In a small suburban village, we waited while the 99ᵗʰ Infantry assaulted the city across an open field. As we waited we were aware of a "ruckus" around a tank parked about a hundred yards away. As the story was told later, a surley German soldier had been taken prisoner, and being unhappy with his situation had boasted, "I can lick any soldier in the American Army." An equally eager tanker had taken up his challenge and they were going at it with bare fists. The tanker proved the German wrong, but I'm sure he left for the POW cage with the satisfaction that he had fought for the Furher to the best of his ability.

As we waited for our orders, a single bullet split the air. Looking toward some tall buildings, I saw the earthworks of several foxholes. Foolishly, as I think of it now, I ran toward the foxholes with my rifle ready. Spotting a "dead" German soldier in one hole I assumed that all was safe and returned to the platoon. I am sure the German was playing "Possum" as I was not impressed with the pallor that is characteristic of dead people. I really took my life in my hands by turning my back on him when I returned to my platoon.

"Tell the men to mount up," Lt. Huff ordered the squad leaders. "We're going into the city. Be prepared to dismount and move in on foot as soon as we come to the first houses. The 99ᵗʰ went in about an hour ago. We'll pass through their lines and take over the assault. Don't expect much opposition, but the report is that some teen age boys are holed up in some street cars and are sniping at everyone in an American uniform."

Our column halted as lead elements entered the edge of the city. My interest turned toward a foxhole near the road that we were on. Several German automatic weapons lay on the dirt surrounding the hole and the body of a soldier was evident from my position in the machine-gun turret. I amused myself by looking at the soldier over the sights of the water cooled machine gun. The driver of the half-track ahead of us, T/5 Marion, was out of his vehicle, minus his helmet and weapon and moving toward the foxhole with the obvious intent of obtaining one of the automatic weapons which lay nearby. Suddenly, he reached for the P-38 pistol in the holster on his belt and moved menacingly toward the foxhole. "Upstanden mitt der hande hohe," he shouted, pointing the pistol into the hole. Three obviously unhappy German soldiers in camouflage suits stood to their feet with their hands behind their heads. They were angry and their faces reflected complete dislike for the situation as it had developed for them. In another hour it would have been dark and they could have made their way into the city where it would have been easy to fade away into the civilian population or to have joined with their own forces and continued their fight to protect the homeland."

I had never heard of the city of Ludwigshaven, but here we were about to enter one of Hitlers major cities. Evidence of war was minimal to the eye. Most of the buildings were still intact and the public transportation system seemed to be operable as evidenced by the street car rails and electric overhead power cables.

It was dark when we dismounted our vehicles and formed up in two columns, one on each side of the street. As platoon runner, I was ordered to bring up the rear. As we moved down the blacked out street, a woman came out of a side street, or ally and took my arm. In mixed English and German, she implored me to get some help for her husband who had been severely wounded by the American artillery.

Suspicious of her intent, I threw her off my arm and continued the march down the street.

A bullet smacked into the wall of the building next to me. "Keep an eye on those street cars across the square," Sgt. Manion yelled. "There's a bunch of Hitler Youth that haven't surrendered yet and they'll shoot anyone that they see."

We halted in front of a large apartment building and while we rested in the street, Lt. Huff and T/Sgt. Manion arranged for our billeting for the night. I don't recall the accommodations. I know I didn't have a sleeping bag, so I probably slept on the floor. About midnight, I was awakened by Sgt. Manion. "McGill," he said, "You've been picked to lead a patrol on the Rhine river to contact an outpost of the 99th Division. You'll have an SCR–300 radio and are asked to call battalion every five minutes to report your progress. Your call sign will be Baker One and the password is "Jackpot". The countersign is "Zebra". The river is about a half mile east of here and the 99th outpost is north of the point where you reach the river. I'm not sure how far. They are supposed to be in a bombed out factory. That's all I can tell you. I've picked five men to go with you. Modrow will be carrying the radio. He should be directly behind you so you can report in at regular intervals."

Pfc. Modrow was a veteran of the fighting in North Africa. He had been with the First Armored there and rotated home after the defeat of the famed Africa Corps. Subsequently he had been reassigned to the Twelfth Armored during it's formation at Camp Campbell, Kentucky. His first name was Herbert. I was well aware that he had a tremendous cigarette cough which caused him to hack almost continuously. "Modrow," I said, "If I so much as hear a wheeze out of you tonight, I'll shoot you." Poor Modrow, I hope he didn't think I was serious. I didn't hear a single sound from him for the next two hours.

The patrol proceeded nicely and we eventually came to a railroad yard with quite a few freight cars. Thru the gaps between the freight cars we could see the waters of the mighty Rhine. We were not about to cross the tracks, but kept the train between us and the river as we were aware that the other side was still in the hands of the enemy and that any observed movement on our side would undoubtedly bring down a hail of artillery. We passed a bombed out factory building with one solitary light still burning in the basement. The street was now very dark as the buildings were fall and forbidding. We crept, or felt our way silently along the sidewalk. Suddenly, I felt a hard object poking me in the stomach. "Give the password." An American voice ordered. Two more shadowy figures emerged from the darkened doorway. "Jackpot," I answered tremulously. "Zebra," came the countersign. "You guys are lucky we didn't shoot and ask questions later, there's been a lot of prisoners taken in this area tonight."

Indeed, we did feel lucky, and as I opened the microphone on the SCR–300 to report to battalion that we had made contact, I felt proud and much relieved that our "Watch on the Rhine" had been successful.

The next day was uneventfull. No enemy contact had been made and the city was trying to return to it's normal routine. I recall seeing a man in gaudy military uniform standing in the middle of the street and very authoritatively directing traffic, both military and civilian. I had it in mind to run him in as a POW. Anyone with a uniform like that must at least be a general. Turned out that he was a member of the local Police force.

I found, in the process of cleaning out a house for possible snipers, a top hat, which I promptly donned and with a liberated motor bike, went riding down a street. I spotted a row of half-tracks parked on a roadway through a field and was planning to check out the markings to see if they belonged to anyone I knew. Fortunately, I was hailed by another G. I. standing beside the road. "You'd better not go out there, soldier, those half-tracks were just knocked out. They got the front and the last one with artillery and all the guys took off. There's a machine-gun covering the field to take out anyone that tries to recover the vehicles." Another close call caused by my own stupidity.

As we were searching the houses in our billeting area, I came across a man in bed. It was mid-day and no one should be in bed at that hour, I reasoned. "Ich haben der Krank," the man had told me. He looked perfectly healthy to me, but it was just too much trouble to take a prisoner today, even though this mature looking individual could well have been another disenchanted German General. Somehow he informed me that the Burgermeister had told him that it would be okay for him to stay in bed.

In the process of going through another house, I spotted a container with milk in it. The cream had risen to the top making it look like the most desireable libation I had had since leaving the States. I made a mental note of it, but since the rest of the squad was with me I was too embarrassed to take a drink. There was no one in the house when we cleared it, but when I went back later in the afternoon, there were people in another room. I could hear them talking as I silently slipped into the kitchen and without ceremony raised the container to my mouth and savored the first real milk I had tasted since the States. I bet the civilians were wondering, "What else will these Americans do? They bomb our cities, defeat our Army, and now they drink our milk!!"

We had taken many prisoners. I had not as much as fired my rifle since coming to town, but the prisoners kept coming. I would give my rifle to one of the other men and go in amongst the prisoners and frisk them for weapons. I had also stooped to taking some of their personal possessions, such as watches and rings. I would never take a wedding ring or their money, but watches were another story. As I was going though the pockets of a number of soldiers and relieving them of loot, one of the men took out a gold encrusted partial bridge and offered it to me. Embarrassed, I shook my head and refused it. From that point on I was much less callous in my searching of prisoners.

One day as we were busy clearing another part of town, we were held up as the 99th Infantry moved through us to take over the assault. Evidently there was opposition up ahead and whoever was in charge of this operation felt that walking Infantry was better qualified to handle it. The relieving infantry was impressive as it moved down the street with the company commander and his staff boldly at the head of the two columns. They had not gone far when two German soldiers with hands lifted came toward them down the street. All at once a shot rang out and one of the surrendering soldiers fell to the street, shot from behind by one of his own men. The second soldier stood dazedly looking down at his buddy, not knowing where to turn or where he should go. We knew now that German soldiers had it worse than we. They had enemy guns in front of them and their own guns behind them. They had little choice but to stand and fight.

It was time to move on. With Lt. Huff in the lead and me directly behind, we moved in two columns down the street. Artillery had been dropping sporadically all morning and as we passed a war damaged building a round landed in it. There was a terrific explosion and the sound of escaping gas. An unfamiliar odor filled the air. Someone shouted, "Gas!!" Terror filled our hearts as we realized that this was the thing we had been trained for and drilled in over and over. No one had a gasmask. The masks had long since been removed from their carriers and deposited, who knows where, in our vehicles. The carriers were now filled with grenades and field rations, which, to us was a much better choice in the kind of war we were fighting. So the chemical warfare people were right after all. Germany still was intent on a final effort to thwart invasion by use of lethal gas.

Someone said, "That smells like ammonia. I think the shell just hit someone's air conditioner." This quelled our anxiety somewhat and since no-one was evidencing any signs of what we had been told we could expect from poison gas, the columns continued on down the street. All were thanking their lucky stars that this was not the real thing and making a mental note to find their gas masks at the earliest convenience.

A few days earlier, Lt. Huff had admonished a group of us to straighten out the pins that held the handles of our grenades on "safe". Most of us had ignored his advice and made sure that the pins would not fall out at an undesirable moment.

As we proceeded down the street, I was next in line behind Huff. T/Sgt Manion was directly across from me at the head of the second column. All at once there was a "crack" that sounded like a rifle bullet. Most of the men were flat on their bellies in the gutters when Manion shouted, "It's a grenade Huff. In your pouch!!" Lt. Huff was now running away from us. I'm sure he realized that if his grenade exploded, that some of us would be injured. As he turned a corner to get behind a building, there was an ugly flash of orange fire and the sound of the grenade exploding. A second grenade was blown across the street where it too exploded. We were all stunned. This had not been due to enemy action, but a tragic turn of events in a war where the unpredictable often happened.

I was first to reach the Lieutenant as he lay in a pool of blood. He was still conscious and as I came up to him, he reached out to me as if to shake my hand. "I'm going boy." He said shakily. "Oh no Huff. You'll be allright." I assured him. "There's been people hurt worse that this and survived."

The pool of blood was spreading at an alarming rate, and as we rolled the wounded man over on his stomach, we could see that one cheek of his buttox was completely missing. Several small veins were spurting streams of blood with each heart beat. The Lieutenant was quiet now and a medic appeared from nowhere with his aid kit. Opening a container of Sulfa he generously sprinkled a layer on the open wound. This was followed by a large gauze pad that completely covered the damaged area. Summoning a Jeep with a stretcher rack, the medics loaded him on the stretcher and proceeded to put the stretcher on the Jeep. Unceremoniously the Jeep drove off with one of the best leaders a soldier could ask for. As my platoon Sgt. and later as my Lieutenant, he had tried his best to make good soldiers of his men. It was a tough job, but I always felt that he liked his men and would always go out of his way to assure our welfare.

Later that evening, we were given the sad news that our Lieutenant had died on his way to the Aid Station.

The hardest thing I remember about Lt. Huff was the time another platoon member and I returned from attending battalion chapel. We met Huff as we came into out bivouac area and he asked. "Where have you guys been?" "We went to chapel down at Battalion headquarters." I responded. "Chapel aye?" he scoffed. "I don't believe that there is a God. Well, maybe I do. I just haven't had time to think about it." I'll never forget these words. They haunt me to this day. I was twenty years old and this man had been like a mother and father to me. I guess I really loved him.

I cannot recall the conclusion of our stay in the city of Ludwigshaven, but I do recall that once the city was secure, we loaded into our half-tracks and headed back the direction we had come from to the city of Kaiserslautern.

As we exited the city we were directed to out knocked out half-track. "Erma" as the vehicle was named after Ryfinski's girl-friend, was a sorry sight. 20 millimeter impacts showed all up and down the right side. Holes were burnt though the armor plate where Panzerfausts had been fired after we had exited. The floor plates were buckled, probably from a German potato masher grenade that was thrown before they dared enter to begin their souvenir hunt. Our bed rolls and clothing were still aboard, but my collection of souvenirs and the picture of Grace that she had sent me as a Christmas present was missing. I was irritated that the enemy took things that meant alot to me.

As our column headed westward, the sun was bright and spring was definitely in the air. Instead of fresh air, it was fetid with the smell of rotting flesh. No bodies were evident, but the smell was definitely that of earlier casualties. We were glad to be headed to a place where we might be able to get a few days rest.

Our quarters in Kaiserslautern were outstanding. We were billeted in a Catholic monastery, or school. Our particular room had a large picture window and a beautiful grand piano.

Directly across the street was a champagne warehouse where Lt. Hune had set up his C. P. Before the good Lieutenant got organized, the troops had busied themselves by liberating cases of champagne and "Sparkling Burgundy." When Lt. Hune realized what was happening, he said, "That's it. No more booze." I was standing nearby when a jeep stopped in front of the building and it's driver approached Hune. "Colonel Wells sent me down to pick up a case of Sparkling Burgandy," he explained. "Oh what's the use?" Lt. Hune exclaimed in frustration. From that point on the goods flowed freely.

Along toward midnight, I was standing my second shift on guard as noone else was sober enough to relieve me, when the sound of an approaching aircraft was heard. Soon after the plane passed, there was a crash in the woods on the hill behind the monastery. I waited for the sound of an exploding bomb, but none ever came. This was either a dud bomb or a supply drop to enemy soldiers holding out in the area behind us. The next day, a patrol got into a pretty hot fire fight with some enemy troops on the hill. The engagement did not involve us, luckily, as most of our unit had a bad overhang.

The next day we found ourselves on the road again. "We've got a pontoon bridge over the Rhine near Worms." Sgt. Manion informed us. "We'll be going back into the Seventh Army as soon as we get across." That sounded okay to us. We'd had quite a journey with the Third Army, having traveled farther and faster in enemy territory than we ever thought possible. I'm not sure, but I think some of our columns did set some new records for armored movement. I guess we proved old Gen. Patton right when he said that we'd have fewer casualties when we kept moving than if we took it slow and cautiously.

The crossing of the Rhine was uneventful. We were cautioned to keep an accurate distance between us and the vehicle ahead and to hold our speed at a certain rate to prevent setting up a harmonic that might wreck the bridge. Engineers were stationed at regular intervals along the treadway, standing in the inflated rubber pontoons that supported it. They would signal the drivers to speed up or slow down as necessary to keep the proper spacing.

Leaving the bridge, we emerged onto a flat area between the river and some distant hills. Here we parked for a couple of hours, assumadly for the brass to collect their thoughts and get all their plans straight. We took advantage of the lull to catnap and eat our noon rations. When the order came to pull out, things went about the same as when we were with General Patton. We would barrel though towns with guns blazing, keeping any would be snipers at bay. "The Infantry will mop up the straglers," we were often told. Whether they did or not, we could have cared less. After shooting up one town pretty bad, our task force commander decided that we were on the wrong road. Finding a wide spot to turn around wasn't an easy task, but eventually we did and came roaring back though the town that we had just riddled. I imagine the civilians were looking for a German column to be in hot pursuit.

Night fell and the column continued to move with "cat-eyes" on. It was impossible to see past the next vehicle ahead. That vehicle belonged to S/Sgt. Robert Edwards. The vehicle was driven by T/5 John Littler. Riding with the mortar squad, lead by S/Sgt. Gene Sabin, I was standing in the ring mount beside him when Edwards vehicle erupted in a sheet of flame. I don't recall hearing a loud explosion of any sort, but there may have been. Members of Edwards squad came running back. I recall that Myers and McCaw were among them. "Get this half-track turned around right now." Sgt. Edwards implored. "We must have taken the wrong turn-off back there. We couldn't see the vehicle ahead and took the most likely looking road. I don't know what hit us, probably a bazooka, but it could have been a mine or an anti-tank gun. I think Littler is dead and I know Vandertie got hit in the leg." T/5 Van Landingham, our driver was turning the vehicle around. The half-track behind us was pulling a trailer and was having a bad time, due to the urgency of the situation, making his turn. We were not real comfortable sitting there waiting for him to move out either as we expected momentarily for the ambushers to make a move on us.

As I recall we got sorted out and rejoined our task force eventually. Next day we were stopped on a road leading though a woods. Looking through the trees we could see several wagons parked. No horses or drivers were visible. Someone thought that this would be a good time to do a little target practice and fired a round into the nearest wagon. To our surprise and delight, a fairly large explosion resulted. This started off a flurry of small arms fire into the innocent looking rolling stock, that resulted in several explosions with highly amusing results. It was like a county fair shooting gallery. To our surprise, a group of about twenty green clad enemy soldiers emerged from the woods a few yards ahead of the wagons that we were busily amusing ourselves with. Hands in air they were ready to call it "Quits". They must have thought that we were shooting at them.

That night, I was sleeping peacefully on the warm deck plates between the driver and the car commander, when a real shoot-out started outside our vehicle. Sabin fired a few rounds from the .30 caliber machine-gun and the tanks ahead of us were having a ball. "What's going on?" I inquired sleepily. "We're shooting up a train," replied Sgt. Sabin. "The road runs right along beside the railroad track and we caught up with it." I could hear the escaping steam, but sleep was more important right now and I didn't bother to look outside.

Early the next morning, the sun was shining brightly. Our task force must have been at least ten miles long. The tanks and Infantry vehicles, interspersed with "flack wagons" from the 572nd Anti-aircraft battalion were in the lead and had passed though a village in a valley and proceeded up a steep highway that fell in the shadow of a fairly high mountain. The artillery, Engineer and other supporting units were on the sunny side of the valley and were visible from our location on the mountain. Field Marshall Goering must have thought this would be a good time for his boys to get in a few good licks before our air force was up and about. Several flights of ME-109's spotted out support vehicles on the bright side of the valley, and with little adoo set about the grim job of disposing of as much of our fighting might as possible. There must have been at least twenty enemy planes and as they peeled off and came at our column in pairs. I could see their bullets impacting in the fields alongside the vehicles. When under air attack, it is standard procedure for all personal, except the gunner to exit the vehicles and disperse in whatever cover the countryside affords. I found myself alone on the .30 caliber water cooled machine-gun. (minus the water) I was baffled to see the enemy planes staffing what appeared from this distance, empty fields. It was not till later that I realized that those dirty dogs were shooting up the troops when they could have been making our task a lot more difficult if they had shot up the vehicles. A task force can't do much damage when their trucks carrying gasoline and rations can no longer keep up. As the first pair of staffing Messerschmidts pulled up to regroup, they were directly overhead of the tanks, half-tracks and flack-wagons. Since this portion of the column was in the shade of the mountain and the pilots were flying directly into the sun, our gunners had a hayday. I was frantically firing the .30 caliber machine-gun and watching the tracers burn out without reaching halfway to the planes. Two tankers on the vehicle behind me were fighting over who was going to fire their .50 caliber gun. I was too shook to think about arguing with anyone and just kept firing to keep up my nerve. I saw the wing of a fighter separate from the fuselage directly overhead as our 40, or 60 millimeter anti-aircraft guns found their target. No parachute appeared and the plane crashed out of sight on the far side of the mountain. It took several minutes for the wing to come flopping to ground. As the planes continued to strafe and our gunners continued to shoot, several more were hit and plunged out of control to the ground. At least four were destroyed, and perhaps more, before they decided that this wasn't a safe place to be and returned to their home field to mend the holes in their planes and count their casualties. To me, the staffing was one of the most nerve shattering experiences of the war. I suppose it was because the planes were visible, while bullets and shells are not. At any rate, whenever I heard the sound of an airplane engine, for the rest of the day, I would cringe and get all tight inside.

As we rolled through the countryside, with little opposition, we would spot enemy ground forces dug in on a hillside, but the task force would take a route that would avoid confronting the enemy and "Just let them be for the walking Infantry to mop up."

Our artillery spotting planes, Dog-4, or Dog-5, were continually up and ahead of us on clear days. Their presence gave us unbounded comfort as we were confident that we could not possibly run into any sizeable enemy concentrations unawares. These guys were good and they saved us a lot of losses that otherwise might have overtaken us.

One day we passed through a large body of green clad, unarmed German soldiers sitting sedately by the road. It seemed kind of erie to be in the midst of hundreds of the enemy and not be shot at. There must have been at least a Battalion. Happily, they no longer wanted to fight. The young soldiers eyed us curiously. For the most part, they were well dressed and clean shaven. They must have been wondering how such a rag tag bunch as we were could cause so much trouble for their forces.

Later that afternoon, word was passed back that there was a strong road-block up ahead and that the Infantry was to dismount and attack on foot.

"Get your guys lined up in two columns, attack formation," Lt. Hune ordered. "Mortar squad, bring your weapon, we may want to use it."

We had no idea where we were going. Like good soldiers we followed our leader. Up a steep hillside to a flat plateau where we stopped and rested a bit. It had been quite a climb for the troops carrying the machine gun, mortar and their associated parts as well as ammo. Looking down over the side of this plateau to the fields below, we were interestedly watching a farmer plowing his field with a horse and oxen. The unevenly matched team was making progress slowly when the driver spied us on the hill. He stopped the team and leaving them standing in the midst of the field took off at a brisk pace in the direction that we assumed the road block and ambush would be. A chorus of shouted "No"s from the troops soon convinced the farmer that his efforts to warn the enemy of our approach might be fatal to him. Turning in his tracks, he walked back to his waiting team. We didn't pause long enough to watch him return to his plowing. "Let's go!" Lt. Hune ordered, and our little task force proceeded in the direction of the alleged strong point.

The flat portion of the plateau was probably a short mile in length, and ended abruptly in a steep decent into a town with a couple dozen houses and outbuildings. "Sabin, set up the mortar here." ordered Lt. Hune. "Sgt. Petrin will lead the assault squad into town. I want you to fire a rolling barrage in front of his lead scout." I'm not sure, but this is probably the first time that the third platoon mortar squad fired their mortar in combat. They had carried this cumbersome instrument of war all through the maneuvers in

Tennessee, training in Camp Barkley, and now for about four months in sporadic combat with our enemy. I think the only rounds fired were in practice.

As the scout, about a hundred yards ahead of the skirmish line made up of the second squad advanced toward the village, the first round was dropped down the tube of the 60mm. mortar. We were surprised to see the scout hit the dirt just nanoseconds before the shell exploded about ten yards to his right. "You'd better not fire any more of them," the Lt. said, "Someone might get hurt."

By now the skirmish line was entering the outer fringes of the little town and we were moving in behind them. Not a hostile shot had been fired at us, but the advancing troops had made their intentions known by shooting out the windows of several buildings. No where to be found were the troops manning the roadblock. No doubt they had seen the probability of being cut off by our attack and had left for healthier environs.

"McGill, take half the third squad and run a patrol south of town. We don't want any surprises while we're waiting for our vehicles to come up." Sgt. Manion was giving the orders. The other half of S/Sgt. Edwards squad was to patrol in a different direction. "Okay you guys, let's go find those Krauts, they must be around here somewhere." I said encouragingly. Actually, I was trying to figure out a course that was least apt to lead us to a spot with enemy soldiers. As we approached a wooded hillside, I told the men following me to remain dispersed and prone while I charged to woods. No one here, so I waved the rest of the group to follow me. We covered quite a bit of ground on that patrol without encountering any signs of enemy activity. Upon our return to the CP I was met by Sgt. Petrin, who asked me to accompany him on a search for a suspected sniper. I hadn't been shot at, but apparently someone had. "You cover me McGill, I'm going to fire this here bazooka into that there chicken coop. If there's any snipers in there, we're sure to get them," he asserted. Darkness was falling fast, and as we cautiously approached the chicken coop, there was no sign of hostile occupancy. The chickens, if there were any, seemed content. Apparently they were not disturbed by any unwelcome guests. We were both fully exposed now, Petrin with his bazooka and me with my M-1. There was a flash as the propellant charge of the rocket ignited and a satisfying and resounding explosion as the war-head exploded in the chicken coop. There no flurry of cackling, nor any death crys of chickens as chickens reacted to the impact of the explosion. No wounded and terrified German soldiers emerged either. "Must have got him." Petrin said. "Let's go back to the CP." The conquering heros returned.

In the darkness, we reported back to Lt. Hune who had found a comfortable bed in the house he had chosen as a C P, and bone weary, as all of us were, was half asleep when someone came in with the report that tanks were heard approaching. "Are they ours?" the sleepy Lt. asked. "We dunno," was the answer. "They might be Krauts." A chill went down my back as I envisioned facing a force of German Infantry supported by several Tiger tanks in this small village that we had just "liberated." "Well, send someone out to see if they are ours or theirs. Tell Manion I said to." This was all we heard from the Lt. as sleep was overtaking him.

I don't recall who made the contact with the tanks, but he soon returned with the report that they were ours and that they would soon be in our village which gave us a great feeling of security.

A good nights sleep makes a lot of difference in the way a soldier looks at life. For one thing, he knows that he has made it though another day and as long as body and soul are still together, life is good. That was the way things looked the next morning when a somewhat rested platoon of Infantrymen found their half-tracks and moved out to face a very uncertain future in the land of the Nazi mad man who had planned to take over our lives and our world.

1. Crossed The Rhine near Worms about March 21st
2. Battle For Nassig, March 31st
3. Wounded in action, April 1st, Easter Sunday

Chapter VII

ATTACK ON NASSIG

D usk was falling as the wheels and tracks of the task force (I believe task force Power) came to a halt on a narrow black topped road. Treeless rolling hills on either side of the road obscurbed the view of the country side. Ahead shells were falling on a nameless country village.

"Post a one man guard on the gun and let your men get some rest." It was T/Sgt. Manion speaking. "D-company is going to attack the town as soon as the artillery lifts. G-2 tells us that it is defended by a training battalion made up of young boys."

It was Friday, March 30th, 1945. Our task force had been on the move since the middle of March, when we spear-headed the Third Army drive to the Rhine at Ludwigshaven. We had lost two of our platoons' half-tracks during that time and the survivors were now riding in the four remaining vehicles. Strangely, we were not crowded. The list of casualties had grown to allow enough vacancies to accommodate us quite well.

As I dozed in the back of our vehicle, surrounded by six or seven of my comrades, I heard a violent argument going on outside. One of the D-company doughs was protesting his orders to join the attack on the village. Their voices rose and fell until finally the officer or non-com involved, prevailed and they marched off to join the others.

A few hours later, it must have been near midnight, I heard my name called from the road outside our vehicle. It was Sgt. Manion again. "McGill, the attack by D-company was repulsed. The Krauts were dug in in the back yards of the houses and when the G.I.'s pushed down the streets they shot Hell out of them. The artillery is in the process of knocking the town down, but the Krauts are digging in outside in the open field between us and the town. We need two patrols, one combat and one recon. You can go with whichever one you choose." Ever since I lost my Half-track to a German 20MM Anti-Aircraft gun a week or so earlier, I had been acting as the platoon runner. The three surviving enlisted men in my squad had been given to other squad leaders to fill in their ranks.

Naturally, I chose the reconnaissance patrol, as I had no particular desire to tangle with the enemy that night. Sgt. Szymoniak was to take a light machine-gun squad to within firing range and harass the entrenching Germans.

The recon patrol, under Staff/Sgt. Sabin, was to find a safe route for the task force to bypass the village and it's defenders.

"The artillery will cease fire on the south half of the town at 0100, so that you will be safe as you may want to get close to the outskirts," Manion informed us.

"O.K. You guys," Sgt. Sabin shouted to his squad. "Let's fall in, I want McGill up front, he carries an M-1. I'll bring up the rear." I was startled by the order for me to lead the patrol, but pleased to be in charge.

"Up the hill to our right seems to be the best route," I reasoned. I wanted to put as much space between us and the town as possible, knowing that the enemy would have listening posts in the vicinity and to keep out of the light thrown off by the burning buildings. The town, by this time was well enveloped by flames which leaped fifty to a hundred feet in the air and gave off an erie reddish light.

As we moved up the hill, spread out in tactical formation, we passed through a line of foxholes. In one, the still form of its occupant was visible in the light from the burning town. He was crouched in a shallow foxhole, with his weapon lying on the parapet before him. He appeared to be dressed in civilian clothes. Possibly a member of the Home Guard or Volkstrom. The most significant thing that I will never forget, about him, was that the top of his head was missing. Our artillery had done it's job even before we arrived on the scene.

Moving through the country side, a hill between us and the town cut off the light from the fires. It was now quite dark. The artillery had lifted and except for an occasional sound of harassing fire on the far side of town, the night was quiet.

Up ahead appeared a vast pit of some kind. We concluded that it was a gravel pit. It's sides were quite precipitous. Just the kind of obstacle an armored force wouldn't want to stumble on in the dark.

As we circumnavigated the pit and moved on, we were suddenly challenged by a weak and distant "Halt!" It sounded like it came from a city block, or so, away. Giving the arm signal to stop and get down, the patrol sank silently to the damp sod. We lay quietly for about five minutes waiting to see what would develop. No further challenges were forth coming, so we rose cautiously from our positions and moved silently forward. Our challenger probably faded away as well and went back to his unit to report what he had seen or heard.

We had now been out about an hour and had traveled about two miles when we began to hear the sound of many voices and the rattle of carts on a road. We concluded that we had now come to the main highway leading out of town that had been pointed out on Sgt. Manions map. The traffic we were hearing was that of the residents whose homes were burning, or theatend, leaving town.

The walk back to the task force was uneventful. "Col._____(name forgotten), would like to talk to you, McGill," Sgt. Manion informed me. "He wants to find out how your patrol went." My heart stopped.

I wasn't used to talking to colonels, let alone a task-force commander. ??? quaked when ever I talked to my own captain. This was different. I had some vital information that our leader needed and I had no choice but to comply.

I found the colonel, (Lt. Col.) very kind and understanding. Standing on the back of his tank and talking to him as he stood in the turret was like speaking to any other soldier who is intent on doing his job. "How'd it go Sgt.?", he asked. "Did you find any enemy or road-blocks?" "No Sir.", I replied, "But we were challenged once and there is a horrendous gravel pit that we'll have to steer around." "Would you be able to lead the task force around the town, if we decide to by-pass it?" He asked. "Yes Sir." I answered. "I'm sure I could follow the same route we took." "O.K., Sgt., Thanks for the information. I'll send a runner for you if we decide to go that way."

Saluting in the dark, I slid down off the tank and made my way back to our half-track where the rest of the squad was already sleeping.

Saturday morning, March 31st. Dawn broke clear and crisp. After a breakfast of "K" rations, I took my turn standing guard on the turret mounted machine gun. The tankers were awake. A 6X6 truck loaded with Jerry cans of gasoline was being unloaded ahead of us. The Quartermaster was hurriedly handing can after can to the tankers who were emptying them in a funnel that lead to the voluminous tank hidden somewhere within the bowls of the thirsty monster. The reason for their haste was the occasional bullets that snapped ominously close. A sniper had, no doubt, positioned himself strategically during the night and was now trying his luck on targets of opportunity.

On the left, on a knoll, about a hundred yards from our road, a black graves registration soldier was busily sewing the body of a fallen comrade into a mattress cover. This was standard procedure for preparing the dead soldiers for burial.

Time passed. The refueling operation was finished. The empty 6 X 6 truck had retreated to the rear to begin the long drive back to a fuel dump at some unknown location behind us.

As I stood in the gun turret, I heard loud cheers from the tanks and half-tracks ahead. The forms of two running soldiers appeared in the ditch beside the road. The leading soldier was dressed in the grey uniform of the Whehrmacht, while the second man wore the bedraggled uniform of the U. S. Army. As the two jogged by, it was clear to see that the German was in real trouble. Blood was spurting from a bullet hole in his wrist. The G. I. was intent in finding help for him before he bled to death. The observing Infantry men were cheering to see an enemy in an awkward position. Right or wrong, we were all rather callous in those days. A bit further down the line I saw a Medic step out from the column and unceremoniously assist the wounded man to a prone position and apply a tourniquet.

Around noon, Sgt. Manion informed us that we were going to take the town. "The line of departure will be the edge of_____, the little village about two kilometers west of the objective," he said. "First platoon will be the assault platoon and the Third platoon will follow. Lt. Hune is in command, B-Co., 43rd tank battalion will support the attack, but will stay behind the Infantry, firing over our heads into the enemy positions and the edge of town. Dismount your men and be ready to move out on foot at 1400 hours."

By three P. M., (1500 Hrs.) we were in position on the edge of town, waiting for orders to begin the attack. The tanks were taking up their position in front of us. The plan was for the infantry to pass through the line of tanks and press the attack with their support from behind.

A pale faced and shaking soldier from the First platoon, obviously shaken by the prospect of the battle, somehow engaged me in conversation. "McGill," he said, "This is suicide." "Don't worry," I replied, "This won't be any different than the dozens of skirmishes we've been through. You'll be okay." A few minutes later the soldier was dead. His name was Donald Caldwell. I don't know where he was from, but his premonition was very accurate.

"Here we go." Sgt. Manion shouted. Already the doughs from the First platoon were moving out in approach march formation, with two squads abreast. As we passed through the line of tanks, the advancing soldiers were very quiet, each with his own thoughts. "Keep your fannies down!" or "Good luck!" from a tanker or two. The pace was brisk with an occasional shout from a squad leader to "Close it up," or "Keep it spread out," we move steadily toward the ominous village whose name we didn't even know. Later we were told that it was Nassig.

We're running now. Bullets are beginning to snap around us. The tanks behind us are firing streams of tracers over our heads and to our flanks. There are foxholes to our right and to our left. We have breached the main line of resistance! Up ahead the town is burning furiously.

The signal to hold up is passed back and we throw ourselves on the ground. Looking around, I see nothing but the dirt thrown up around enemy foxholes. No way to tell if they are occupied. A head emerges from a hole to my left. No Helmet. The owner seems to be surveying the situation. I have never been this close to a living target before. I hesitate, since a shot now would be about two inches above the rump of Pfc. Dentino. "I'll never tell," I thought and centered the head on the front post and squeezed the trigger. The bullet impacted the ground about a hundred yards beyond the target. "It's this new rifle that Captain Shoemaker gave me the other night when we passed him beside the road." I reasoned. I hadn't bothered to sight it in since Capt. Shoemaker had assured me that it was an excellent piece, and that according to the Geneva Convention he was not allowed to have it in his possession. (Capt. Shoemaker was the Battalion Surgeon assigned to our task force.) I lowered my aim and took a second shot. This time the head disappeared like magic.

The column was moving again. I saw Pfc. Leonard Zappa, white as a sheet, convulsing on the ground as we passed. He had taken a pistol shot in the chest and to all appearances, was dying. To our joy, we later learned that he survived.

First platoon to the left, Third platoon straight ahead. We were on the outskirts of town. Lt. Hune had assembled most of the Third platoon in the shelter of a large machine shed. As we watched, he pulled the pin on a grenade and ran around the corner of the building, lobbed it into a foxhole and returned in great haste. He repeated this two or three more times and then, ordering Sgt. Frank Szymoniak to accompany him, proceeded into the field about fifty yards and brought in a wounded soldier.

As I looked back across the smoky field through which we had just come, I saw that it was littered with bodies. I couldn't believe my eyes. I hadn't seen anyone except Zappa as we passed through, but there they were. The Medics were already picking up the wounded. A Jeep with two stretchers was moving among the prone figures. Two of them were afoot and were examining each body for signs of life. I resolved at that moment that they couldn't pay me enough to go back out and do what they were doing. I've never met a Medic that I didn't like.

"Okay, we're going into town!" Lt. Hune shouted. "Keep your eyes open for snipers in the upper story windows. We'll stay in contact with the First platoon be radio. They'll be going up a street parallel to ours."

Looking over my shoulder, as we moved out, I could see that the tanks were advancing across the field and would be entering the town close behind us.

We're ruining again, weaving from side to side, hitting the pavement, rolling over to spoil the aim of a would-be assassin. I'm firing into the dirt around a foxhole across the street. If anyone is in it, I don't want him popping up now. The smoke from burning buildings is blinding us and making the outline of buildings ahead unclear. There is a white cow lying in the vacant lot across from us. She has been hit by shrapnel and is in agony. She is moving her head to her side and back. Taking aim, I fire at her head, hoping to put her out of her misery, but more to occupy my mind, as I feel as big as an elephant lying immobile in the gutter. "Hold your fire, McGill," Sgt. Sabin shouts, "Some of our guys might be in those foxholes!" Ridiculous!!

"Let's go!!" Sgt. Sabin is up and moving. At a trot we move through the village without incident. The town is deserted. Neither soldier or civilian is to be seen.

Finding a house intact, we move in. An elderly woman, all dressed in black is in the kitchen. She is obviously shaken and when no-one makes a move on her, she looks unsteadily at me and asks, "Du nischt sheisen?" She obviously had been told that any civilians that stayed behind would be shot by the attackers. I must have looked pretty foreboding, with a weeks growth of beard, two bandoleers of ammunition and an array of grenades hanging from my untidy and disheveled uniform. It would be enough to make anyone wary. I smiled. "Nischt sheisen." Her face lit up and she smiled a toothless smile. Indeed, we all felt better. Her smile and her tearful Danke, danke." did a lot to relieve the tension of the battle that we had just survived.

We posted a one man guard, while the rest of us tried to relax in the comfort of the home. We found some food items in the pantry and made short work of them.

Eventually Sgt. Manion arrived. "Congratulations, you guys. You did a great job out there today. Your half-track will arrive shortly."

The battle for Nassig is over!! Tomorrow is Easter Sunday!!

Chapter VIII

HETTSTADT-FINIS LA GUERRE

Easter Sunday broke with bright sunshine and a cool breeze from the west. Before sunrise the tankers and infantrymen of our task force were awake and preparing for another day of travel and action against what seemed to be stiffening resistance by a stubborn enemy.

We had spent the night coiled up with the tanks in an opening in the woods beside the road which we had traveled following the battle at Nassig on the previous day. The exhilaration of a battle won had now somewhat subsided and the anticipation of further action on this day, the first of April, was having a sobering affect.

The order to "Mount up", was given and the task force slowly uncoiled and emerged from the bivouac area onto the road leading to our next scene of action.

About ten o'clock we entered a wooded area and dispersed the vehicles to avoid crowding in case of artillery attack. Up ahead the sky was filled with the black puffs of smoke put up by countless German Ack-ack guns, as flight after flight of P-47s dove and bombed unseen targets. It was obvious to all that we were now approaching a main line of resistance which the enemy had not been able to establish up until now

As the P-47s continued their strafing and bombing attack, two P-51s, appeared out of nowhere and decided to get in on the action. After just one strafing pass, one of the newcomers pulled up over our position with smoke trailing. An orange patch of fire was seen on the planes right wing. As the pilot climbed for altitude, we observed the ejection of his canopy. The canopy was followed shortly by the pilot. His chute opened and as he was falling, he was furiously "dumping" his chute to guide him into the woods where friendly troops were standing by. The strong westerly winds at that altitude were blowing him irresistibly toward the German lines.

As the pilot, and his chute, was about to land, someone ordered a Jeep to go out and pick him up. The unfortunate airman was now on the ground, in an open field, and several enemy soldiers were seen taking him prisoner. The Jeep never left our area. It was evident that the enemy was now holding positions within a mile of our own.

As morning turned to afternoon, the troops became restless. The incessant strafing and bombing continued, mixed now with our own artillery directed by the persistent flight of two of our L-5, observation planes. The barrages seemed to be dangerously close and we were all curious to know what they had found that was so worthy of their attention. As we emerged from the woods, later that day, we found out.

As I, and some of the others from Sgt. Edwards squad, wondered about the area, trying to kill time, we came on a gruesome scene. An American light machine-gun, set up and properly loaded, was located at the base of a large tree. Behind the gun, lying face down was a Staff Sgt. from an unknown unit. No bullet wounds were evident, but when I pulled out his dog tags to check his identification, they were covered with blood. Within a few yards were two additional loaded .30 caliber ammunition cans and behind those another pair. It was apparent that when their squad leader was killed, his ammunition bearers had taken leave of the scene and retreated to safer places.

We notified Pfc. Peeler, our platoon radio man, who immediately called for an evacuation vehicle to pick up the fallen soldier.

The afternoon was spent leisurely wondering about the area. At the edge of the woods, by the side of a black-top road, concealed beneath overhanging trees, was an ME-109 mounted on a trailer. The aircraft had probably sustained damage and was being transported back to it's field when caught by American planes. The driver of the prime mover had evidently decided that he could make better time without the cumbersome load, to which he had been assigned, and had unhooked and retreated to a more comfortable location.

"Get the squad together," ordered Sgt. Edwards, "We're going to attack dug in enemy troops between here and the Main river. The tanks will follow the road, and we will be on foot providing protection from snipers and bazookamen. It seems like every soldier in the German Army has a Panzerfaust."

As we moved through the woods in approach formation, two lines abreast, Captain Powers appeared in his Jeep driven by First Sgt. Berry. They drove slowly between the two lines of marching Infantry, looking each man over to see just what shape we were in. I'm sure it was obvious to them that our depleted and exhausted ranks were in dire need of a break. Never the less, our moral was good, and we were ready to do what ever the task happened to be.

As we emerged from the woods, I was overpowered by a strange premonition. "This battle is going to be different from the dozens of engagements we've experienced so far. I'm not going to get out of this like I did from the others." I began to pray. "Dear God, I know I'm not worthy to ask for your protection, but please hear my mothers prayer."

To our left front, at about three hundred yards, stood a battery of four of the dreaded German Eighty-eights. Their muzzles were pointing directly at us, but all about them were the shreds of torn and ripped camouflage nets. Our artillery, with the help of the little spotter planes had done an excellent job, and not a round could have been fired from any of the damaged field pieces.

Soon we were joined by the tanks and we moved together onto the paved road directly into the field of fire of the four now disabled guns. "McGill, take Modrow and Best and clear out that building behind those guns. There may be some of the crew still hiding there." Sgt. Edwards ordered. The building in question was a large two story structure which turned out to house pumping equipment for some unknown water supply. It stood about a hundred yards from the road and in a field devoid of any kind of cover whatsoever. The dash across the open ground was dangerous, but we reached the cover of the building without incident. Kicking in the door, I entered, covered by the guns of Pfc.'s Modrow and Best. The building proved to be empty, except for the large pumps and electric motors and a tangle of various sized pipes, valves and fittings. Peering out through a crack in the shutters that covered a window on the back side of the building, we could see numerous foxholes, but were unable to ascertain if they were occupied.

The task force had now been moving steadily along the road, and assuming that our mission had been accomplished, we now prepared for the hazardous run back to join it. Wishing to give the other two soldiers protecting cover, I sent Modrow out first. Best followed. As he covered the distance to the road, I was somewhat dismayed as I saw small puffs of dirt kicked up where bullets from enemy rifles impacted the soft ground around him. "Oh oh!! Now it's my turn!!" I thought. "Well, here goes." Bending low, and zig-zagging to spoil the enemies aim, I ran at full bore back to the protection of the tanks.

The tanks were firing their big guns now at targets not seen by the ground troops. I was awed to see what I thought was a tarpaulin or shelterhalf thrown into the air when a shell hit a foxhole about two hundred yards away. As I looked the object flew about six feet into the air rotating slowly as in slow motion. It was then that I realized that the object had arms and legs and that it was not a tarpaulin or shelter half at all, but the overcoat of a real live, (probably dead) enemy soldier who still wore it.

Things were getting pretty noisy now. The tanks were firing their large caliber guns and their machine guns. I'm sure that our assault squad, lead by Sgt. Petrin was now under fire. Thus far, I had not had a target. In a lull in the firing, I could hear the sounds of another fire fight just over the hill from us. We had not been aware of another task force that close.

As my squad passed a stationary tank, the commander, a Lieutenant, spotted me. "Sgt.", he shouted in irritation, "I want some dough's in those foxholes on our left flank. That's a direct order." I could see between his tank and the next one. There was a line of uncamouflaged parapets where holes had been dug about a hundred yards from the road. "Yes Sir," I replied. As I think of it now, I should have reported this order to my commander, Lt. Hune. By obeying the tanker, I went AWOL. I had been taught to never disobey an order from an officer, no matter who he was. "Okay, Best and Modrow, follow me." Without hesitation, we took off on a dead run in the direction of the foxholes, not knowing if they were manned or not.

About ten yards from the first hole, we hit the dirt, hoping that any occupants would show their heads. No one appeared. Moving the safety on my rifle to the "armed" position. I rose and charged the nearest hole, firing into the bottom of it as I cleared the parapet. I knew I wouldn't have time to make a decision whether to shoot or not if the hole was occupied. No one home!! What a relief!! Here I was safely situated in an enemy foxhole, with my men still in the open. As I had leaped into the hole, firing from the hip, the brutal recoil of my unsupported M-1 rifle, sent the receiver and rear sight into my chin. I was quite severely cut and bleeding. When Modrow and Best crawled up to my hole and saw the blood, they immediately thought I was mortally wounded, and with one accord took off back to the column and the safety of the tanks.

What to do? Not knowing whether neighboring foxholes were manned, I placed my helmet on my hand and raised it above ground to see if anyone would fire at it. I was even concerned that some of the tankers, in the heat of battle, might not recognize that friendly troops, (me) now occupied the positions on their flank.

After convincing myself that all was safe, and that none of the neighboring foxholes were occupied, I returned to the line of tanks. The run across the open ground was uneventful and I was not aware of being fired at.

As I reached the ditch on the far side of the tanks, the infantry was lying prone, and I joined them in that position. The firing was still heavy, and as I looked ahead, I saw Pfc. McCaw stand and begin firing his rifle in the direction from which hostile fire was coming. He had only been on his feet for a few seconds when I saw dust fly from his clothing about knee high. He spun half-way around and fell to the ground. "Oh, oh, there goes McCaw," I thought.

"McGill," Sgt. Edwards shouted, "Take over the assault squad." "Who, me?" I thought, and prepared to follow his order. (I learned later that Sgt. Petrin had been killed leading the Infantry) At that point, a soldier from one of the other squads, carrying a bazooka, passed me moving toward the rear in great haste. He flopped to the ground directly behind me.

I raised my head and turned to reprimand him. At that point, I felt the most powerful blow I had ever received. I imagined someone with a baseball bat had just laid it on my left jaw and shoulder. I was stunned, I'm sure, and contrary to all the training I had had, I quit soldiering right there. Raising to my knees, and making a great target for a second shot, I removed my left glove and placed it over the hole in my neck from which spurts of blood were raising small puffs of dust where they hit the earth. "My jugular vein is cut," I thought, "Lord, why does death have to come by bleeding to death? Why couldn't the shot have been better placed so I could die immediately?"

To my surprise, the bleeding stopped. A Physician told me later that a muscle in my neck must have moved over the puncture and closed off the bleeding. The pain was terrific. My mouth felt like it was full of teeth and my left arm was paralyzed. As I realized that this might not be the end after all, I returned to the prone position, opened my cartridge belt and crawled backward, leaving all my gear and weapon forever.

Lt. Hune was immediately at my side. I wasn't aware that he was anywhere near me when all the firing was going on, but here he was. Opening my first aid pack, he began to dress the hole in my neck. "Don't worry about me," I said. "Get up front where you belong. They're shooting up our guys." "Get on that tank, they're taking wounded to the rear," he ordered. "I can't," I replied, "my arm is broken." "Get up there anyway," he ordered. With my left arm hanging limp, I made my way toward the tank which was backing past the others still engaged in the battle. I could see several others soldiers on the back of the tank and as I struggled to mount up to join them I recognized Pfc. McCaw and S/Sgt. Edwards, my squad leader.

"Get off my knee, McGill," McCaw complained as I tried to find space over the engine compartment. "Get off my arm," I retorted in some sense of reprisal. The rush of cold air through the grate over the engine felt refreshing, and I'm sure that without it I would have fainted.

It was beginning to get dark now. The last impression I had of the task force was with T/Sgt. Manion, standing on the back of a tank, firing the fifty caliber machine-gun into the enemy positions. I understand that the attack was called off because of darkness and that the objective, the town of Hettstadt, was taken the next day.

It was only a matter of minutes before the tank on which we were riding had put a hill between us and the action. There, to our surprise, was Captain Shoemaker, our battalion surgeon, with an ambulance and his aid station. The medics were busily tending to other wounded when we arrived.

Do you understand now why I have always said, "I never met a medic that I didn't like?" All through our combat days, these dedicated soldiers had shadowed us. Always within a few yards of the action. Many of them right with us. Many of them giving their lives to make sure that their help was there when needed. My hat is off to the Medical Corps of the U. S. Army for their ceaseless and sacrificial attention to our needs.

I thought that I was badly wounded. I sat on the ground pouting. The medics were attending to others who needed their attention worse than me. It began to sink in that I was not so bad off after all.

I had a strange feeling that I was deserting my fellow soldiers. Here they were still in the midst of battle, with no sign of let up, and I am headed to the hospital. "Maybe I will be well soon so I can rejoin them," I thought. It seemed incomprehensible that this could be the end of combat for me. After four long months of constant tension, overcoming fear and experiencing the comradeship of fellow soldiers who were as miserable as I, it was hard to accept the change.

Finally, it was my turn. A medic approached me and with a scissor, cut away my field jacket, shirt, sweater and underwear. After applying a large compress to my shoulder wounds, (There was two of them. Where the bullet entered and where it left.) I was given a shot of morphine and placed on a stretcher. I'll never forget the warm fuzzy feeling of lying on the stretcher while two aid men snugly tucked G. I. blankets around me. This done, a shipping tag was made out and attached to the stretcher stating that I had been wounded at Hettstadt, a place that I had never heard of.

Two Aid Men now grasped the stretcher and began to place it into a waiting ambulance. Three spaces were already occupied. Much to my pleasure McCaw, Edwards and another unknown casualty were my companions.

"Where'd you get hit, McGill?" Sgt. Edwards asked as the ambulance began to move. "I got it in the fanny." There was a chuckle, and as the vehicle gained speed the morphine began to take affect along with many long days and sleepless nights. We all became drowsy.

I remember sometime during the trip asking the Medic, who occupied the seat next to the driver, if I could have a drink of water. I was now suffering from thirst more than from the wounds that I had sustained. "We're not permitted to give our riders water," was the reply, "Someone may have internal wounds that we aren't aware of and water would be detrimental." Sounded reasonable and I resolved to ignore my thirst in deference to policy.

We must have ridden for six or seven hours when the ambulance stopped. After a short discussion between the driver and someone at the new location, the door opened and we felt the cool air of early morning hit our faces. We were quickly unloaded and carried into a large tent lined with cots filled with sleeping wounded.

Enter. An angel. She was dressed in Army fatigues. The coverall type. On her head was an officers overseas cap with a shiny silver bar. A First Lieutenant. From under the cap flowed the most beautiful hair I ever saw. Shining in the dim light. Clean and beautiful. The most gorgeous person I had ever seen. (or was it the morphine?)

"Welcome to tent city, boys." We hung on every word, with open mouths as we watched every move of this unbelievably graceful creature that God had provided to bring us a healing touch. "This is a Field Hospital, and you will only be here a few days. As soon as we have tended your wounds and you are well enough to be moved, you will be flown to a General Hospital in Rheims." With that we watched in awe as she moved gracefully out of sight.

I was given a cot across the aisle from a wounded German soldier. I was in a rather euphoric state of mind, and after being given a stiff drink of brandy mixed with the first milk I had tasted in many days, I was also belligerent. When the soldier continued to moan and complain, I started to do some complaining myself. "Get this gold brick out of here or I'll kill him." I shouted with bravado. "I've just been shot by one of his kind and I don't intend to share my bed with him!!" Well, it didn't take long for the Ward Boys to realize that I might not be bluffing, and before I knew it, two of them grasped my cot and moved me into another tent where I immediately fell asleep.

"Where'd this fellow come from?" Someone was standing close to my cot and looking down on me. As I blinked, I could see dimly the face of a middle aged doctor and a Ward Boy. "Oh he came in a couple of days ago, but he was so out of it we just let him sleep." I have no idea how long I had slept. I do know that my medical records now show that I was wounded on the second of April, and not on the first, Easter Sunday, as actually happened.

The foregoing manuscript may not be the most historically correct account of WWII, but it's the way that I remember it. The long weeks in Army hospitals went rapidly. I missed my comrades at arms tremendously and it was hard for me to believe that this was the end of the war for me. As the French say, "Finis La Guerre."